A
BOOK OF
PUBLIC
PRAYERS

A
BOOK OF
PUBLIC
PRAYERS

By
HARRY
EMERSON
FOSDICK

HARPER & BROTHERS

New York

Contents

Introduction

WHEN THE nonliturgical churches decided to dispense with officially recognized forms of public prayer, and to trust the individual ministers with the responsibility of formulating their own prayers, they took a fateful step. Those clergymen who have been reared in the nonliturgical tradition and who would not feel at home in any other, should be the first to confess the widespread inadequacy of public prayer in their services of worship. The Anglican, with his *Book of Common Prayer,* can be sure, as he goes to church on Sunday, that his gratitude will be expressed, his sins will be confessed, and his petitions will be presented, "decently and in order," with dignity and beauty. In nonliturgical churches, however, the ministers commonly fail their congregations at just that point.

One reason for this is the idea that the reading of a printed prayer can readily become a mere routine procedure—as it undoubtedly can—and that to be genuine a prayer should be spontaneous and extempore. This emphasis on spontaneity, however, neglects the important fact that leading a congregation in public prayer is a work of art, demanding expert skill and painstaking preparation. Extempore spontaneity is not the only alternative to a printed liturgy. The real alternative is thoughtful, careful, skillful preparation.

In nonliturgical churches the minister does not kneel in the chancel, facing the altar, as though addressing himself to the Most High. He stands in the pulpit, facing the congregation. That obvious fact defines his function in public prayer. He is trying so to phrase the soul's adoration, thanksgiving, penitence, petitions, and intercessions, that the people may be caught up into his prayer and may themselves pray with him. That is a sacred, soul-searching task. It calls for deep and sympathetic insight into human need, for sensitive awareness of both individual and social problems, and for faith in God's grace and mercy; and it demands dedicated and careful preparation as much as does the preaching of a sermon.

Certain familiar faults which commonly afflict the so-called "pastoral prayer" in nonliturgical churches can be readily specified. Some prayers are narrowly self-centered, dealing almost exclusively with certain individual needs in the congregation, and lacking any expressed awareness of the world's need, its social tragedies and sins, and any care for the missionary and philanthropic enterprises which serve mankind.

Some prayers deal in vague generalities, and do not come to grips with specific needs. They ask forgiveness for sins, but they do not say what sins. They express gratitude for blessings, but they do not name the blessings. They petition God for the church and the nation, but they do not concretely define what help they are praying for. No wonder that prayer time is often put to somnolent use!

Some prayers are a confused jumble of all sorts of requests, meditations, aspirations, and even homilies, which occur to the extempore pray-er. A public prayer should be an orderly sequence of "collects," in each of which some special adoration, thanksgiving, confession, or supplication finds concentrated expression. Such a well-organized prayer can be followed and participated in by each member of the congregation.

Some prayers are Sunday after Sunday a repetitious rehearsal of the same petitions in much the same words. The congregation knows almost exactly what the minister is going to say in his pastoral prayer. Nonliturgical clergymen have given up the printed prayer book lest it become routine, but all too easily they create their own routine, week after week repeating themselves, using well-worn clichés, until the public prayer becomes to many a verbal formality. It lacks the freshness, radiance, and challenge that genuine prayer should possess.

Indeed, speaking personally, I have felt so seriously the perils that beset the public prayer, and have found the pitfalls so often trapping my own feet, that I have for years resisted

attempts to persuade me to publish a book like this. I surrender now with some hesitation and misgiving. Who can
worthily address the God and Father of our Lord Jesus Christ,
week after week carrying up to him the prayers of the people,
and guiding their worship alike with reverent awe and with
specific petition? Yet we ministers have that responsibility and
opportunity. I offer this book of prayers for public worship
simply as one man's attempt to do the best he knew how.

HARRY EMERSON FOSDICK

PASTORAL
PRAYERS

ETERNAL SPIRIT, who carest for each of us as if thou hadst none else to care for, and yet carest for all even as thou carest for each, we turn our hearts to thee. All our thoughts touch but the outskirts of thy ways; our imaginations are but partial pictures of thy truth; our words concerning thee are short plummets dropped into a deep sea. Yet into thy sanctuary we come with grateful and expectant hearts, because while we, by searching, cannot find thee out, thou, by thy searching, canst find us.

Spirit of the living God, discover us today. Come through the tangled pathways, grown with weed and thicket, that have kept thee from us. We cannot reach to thee; reach thou to us, that some soul, who came here barren of thy grace, may go out, singing, O God, thou art my God!

Discover us in conscience. Let some moral imperative be laid upon our souls today. Save us from our evasions and deceits, and the soft complacency with which we excuse ourselves, and let some ennobling word of justice and beauty come to us today. Be stern with us, O living God, and chasten us by strong guidance in righteousness.

Discover us through the experience of forgiveness. Thou seest how many sins here have never been made right—barbed words spoken that hurt another, never atoned for, and still unforgiven; wrongs done against thy laws and man's good, and no pardon sought, no restitution made. Grant us the salvation of thy forgiveness, and the pardon of those whom we have wronged. May some fellowship gone awry be put straight today; may some broken relationships be restored to integrity; may some storm-tossed souls find thy peace.

Come to us in the spirit of dedication. Never great until we confront something loftier than our own lives, never happy while we are self-centered, we seek our salvation in thee. Bring thou within our ken some purpose worth living for; remind us of some whom we can help, some cause that we can serve. May we forget ourselves into character and usefulness, because thou hast sought us out.

Come to us in the experience of inner power. We ask not for easy lives, but for adequacy. We ask not to be freed from storms, but to have houses built on rock that will not fall. We pray not for a smooth sea, but for a stout ship, a good compass, and a strong heart to sail. O God, discover us with the resources of thy power, that we may be strong within.

We pray for our unhappy world in all its wretchedness and violence. See how our sins have wrecked the peace of mankind, divided us into warring nations and hostile races, and made so unequal man's comfort and estate that the world is rent by envy and ill will. Come thou to thy wayward humanity, all of us thy children, one family with one Father, trying ruinously to be something that we are not, enemies when we should be brothers. Bring the Spirit of the Christ into our hearts, we humbly beseech thee.

On all soldiers of the common good let thy blessing rest. From housewives in the kitchen to presidents and kings in their high stations, we pray for all, in ordinary or extraordinary places, who serve their fellows. Upon physicians and nurses, lawyers and teachers, businessmen and statesmen, upon all who work for the poor and bear on their hearts vicariously the burdens of unhappy folk forgotten by the world, we ask thy blessing. Upon all those who work for the purification of our politics, the bringing in of world peace, and the spread of the Gospel of the Son of Man we pray.

Help us all so inwardly to conduct our own lives that whether we live in prosperity or misfortune we, too, may be among the honorable company of thy true servants who lift the world and do not lean upon it, and who leave it a better place in which thou mayest rear thy human family.

We ask it in the Spirit of Christ. AMEN.

ETERNAL GOD, our Father, high above all yet in all, thy children gather in thy sanctuary to worship thee. Thou fillest the heaven and the earth so that none can hide himself where thou canst not see him. Through all the universe thou flowest like the living blood through our bodies, yet there is one spot where we feel the pulse, where, putting the finger, we know the heart is beating. Let thy sanctuary be that to us this day. O God, who fillest all things, here let us feel the beating of the Eternal Heart.

We pray for thy special grace upon this hour, not for this hour's sake but that all of life may be elevated and strengthened. Make thyself so real to us here that never again canst thou be utterly unreal. Out from this place, where specially we have found thee and been found by thee, may we go never again to lose sight of thee. May our family life be more wholesome, our friendships more faithful, our difficulties borne with more equanimity and fortitude, our bereavements endured with more trustfulness and hope, our work done with better fidelity, honesty, and kindliness, because we have met here.

Take us all into thine embrace. Be with the children that come up from the gates of the morning. Let them not by wrong training, evil example, or disastrous cricumstance be turned away from thy purpose for them. Steady our boys and girls in their tumultuous years amid the waywardness of this generation. Keep their self-respect unsullied. Save them from the contagion of this unclean world, and may they be strong to offer thee valiant service in the years ahead. Be with the mature in the floodtide of their power. Let no prosperity spoil them, no disappointment crush them, no faithlessness overtake them. Keep them true to the knightly vows they took in their chivalrous years, and let their strength be glorified in thy service. Support the aged, now drawing near the river across whose flood they see in vision the shining battlements of the heavenly city. Establish them in their going and give them a triumphant welcome on the other side.

So encompass us in all our varied needs, we pray thee, and in thine everlasting arms enfold us, every one.

We pray for the sensitive and answering spirit and for the listening ear. As the air is full of messages which, unattuned, we do not hear, so is creation filled with words from thee which our dull spirits miss. Save us this day from living like blind men in the midst of beauty not seeing it, like impure souls in the presence of love not comprehending it. Against our dullness, our insensitiveness, our callousness, our thank- lessness, we pray. May we open our hearts to thine incoming, O thou God of righteousness and love.

Give us the victory, we beseech thee, over our doubts. Thou seest with what subtle and dangerous effect they creep upon us, undermining the foundations of character, stripping away the worth from life and leaving us at last with a universe bereft of thee and an existence empty of meaning. Build deep into our hearts faith in thee and thy Christ, and so faith in ourselves, in our race and its possibilities, and in eternal things unseen over which death has no dominion.

For those who labor for the spiritual welfare of the people we pray. Lift up leaders in our time. Give us courage to stand strong against the evils that afflict the souls and societies of men. Against harshness, crookedness, guile, and all chicanery, against uncleanness, hatred, prejudice, and all contempt of personality make us strong to stand, that in our day Christ may see of the travail of his soul and be glad at the progress of his Kingdom.

We ask it in his name. AMEN.

3

ETERNAL SPIRIT, to whom we belong and in whom we live, we worship thee, seeking a fresh consciousness of thy reality and thy penetrating presence. Too often like creatures of the sea we question whether there is any water, like birds upon the wing we ask whether there is air. For, lo, in thee we live and move and have our being, yet we spin long arguments about thine existence and labor our debates about thine attributes. This day we would not debate but experience thee. We would not argue but would know.

We do not pray as though by supplication we could instruct thee concerning our needs, or win thee from forgetfulness as though thou must be reminded or urged. We pray against our own reluctance, not against thine. We would have our hearts opened by our prayers that thou mightest come in, as thou hast long desired.

O God, help us never to lose our vision of thee. Thou art the center and the circumference. Thou bindest together all that is worthy and meaningful in life. Steady our faith in thee; and if some of us here today have been shattered by doubt, hurt by disbelief, until life has been drained of its worth, restore to us such a vision of thee that we may believe triumphantly again.

Beget in us a new love for people. Forgive us that so often we are fatigued by them, worn out by their multitude and the irritation of their demands. Give us grace to see beneath the surface into the hearts of persons, to sympathize more deeply with the needs of human lives, to love better the things that are lovely in people, to excuse more mercifully the things that are unlovely, to mend more helpfully the things that are amiss.

Beget in us a new hatred of sin. Forgive us that we ever by familiarity become accustomed to wickedness until we first tolerate and then embrace it. O God, by as much as we love people may we hate the things that ruin people, that blacken the face of human lives, despoil them of their loveliness and hope, and wreck them like shattered hulks upon the shore. Give us again indignation against things that are base and vile.

Strengthen our churches, we pray thee. For all the benedictions that have come to us from the heritage handed down by the long succession of thy people, we thank thee. Recall to us the memories of earlier days when we were illumined and dedicated because the influence of thy Church was thrown around our youth. God help us to build better churches. Forgive us that they so poorly represent thee. Save us from pettiness, triviality, and sectarianism. Give us grace in efficiency and wisdom, in loyalty and high spirit, to build better churches for our children after us.

O God, bless our country. Upon the President of the United States and all those associated with him in authority let thy benediction rest. Save us from the folly of a haughty spirit and the disaster that follows pride. From all hardness of heart, all trust in violence, all greed of wealth and power, save us, O Lord! In this day, alike of our peril and our opportunity, lift us up to be a force for freedom, for righteousness, for peace, for true religion among the peoples of the earth.

Beyond the power of any voice to present our varied needs do thou meet them, Spirit of the living God. Gather us into thine everlasting arms, and according to the diversity of our need be the multiplicity of thy supplies, O God of grace and truth!

We ask it in the name of Christ. AMEN.

4

ETERNAL GOD, thou Light that dost not fade, thou Love that dost not fail, we worship thee. We seek thee not because by our seeking we can find thee, but because long since thou hast sought us. We do not seek the sun, but open ourselves to its light and warmth when it arises. We do not seek the fresh air of heaven, but open our windows and, lo, it blows through. So may our hearts be responsive to thy coming and receptive of thy presence.

We have tried to content ourselves with worldly goods. Well housed, well clothed, well fed, we have tried to be satisfied; but within us rises an insatiable desire for a life that is life indeed. Man cannot live by bread alone, and so we turn to thee.

We have tried to satisfy ourselves with sin. We have thrown off the bit and bridle of the moral law, and have sought for ourselves some hell where we might be happy. But, O God, there was no happiness in hell. Thy voice haunts us, crying shame upon us; and all that is worthy and beautiful allures us still, and we come to thee.

We have tried to content ourselves with daily tasks. We have given ourselves to our work and absorbed ourselves in our toil. Yet we wistfully have asked: Is there a divine source behind life, divine meaning in it, divine destiny ahead of it? So we come to thee. From all endeavors to live without thee we return evermore to thee.

Take our lives into thy keeping and transform them. Take our sins into thy hands. We are ashamed of them. Yet canst thou not use even them? We ask not simply that thou wilt forgive our sins, but that thou wilt use them. May they make us more merciful because we confess a common nature with our wayward humanity! May they give us a deeper insight into the needs of human souls, and a quicker cry of gratitude that belongs only to those who have been forgiven by thy matchless grace! Make us more compassionate, more sympathetic, more useful, because thou hast saved us from our sins.

Take our sufferings, we beseech thee. We have rebelled against them and often have been embittered by them. Canst thou not use them? Because of them kindle in our hearts a generous sympathy with the whole body of humanity, since we too have walked with thee through the dark valley and have been comforted there by thy rod and thy staff.

Take our bereavements, we pray thee. Make life eternal more homelike because of friends whom death has taken from us. Let earth lose somewhat of her steadfast hold upon us, and heaven gain a new place in our hope and a new reality in our thought, because some who have walked beside us here have gone to walk with thee upon the shores where the shining ones do commonly congregate.

Take our powers, we pray thee. Lift up our eyes to see the need of this crucial generation. Put our shoulders to the wheel; put our hands to the task. Take the energies that thou hast given us and dedicate them. We would not cling to thee with our weakness only. We would cleave to thee with our strength also. Be thou the God of our powers.

So we beseech thee, Almighty God, that as we thus have come, people of kindred sympathies and common aspirations, to this place to pray, thou wilt do high business in our souls. Mold us, transform us, encourage us, inspire us, empower us.

We ask it in the name of Christ.   AMEN.

5

ETERNAL GOD, so high above us that we cannot comprehend thee and yet so deep within us that we cannot escape thee, make thyself real to us today!

We are tired of our littleness and would escape from the narrow limitations of our ordinary lives. Lift us into the fellowship of the saints in light. From our discouraged thoughts of human nature redeem us by the remembrance of the shining ones, for they too walked the common ways of earth. They too are our brethren and reveal the possibilities of man's nature. Lift us into the companionship of the noble living and the noble dead that in their fellowship our faith may be renewed, our hope strengthened, our courage confirmed.

If thus we seek high fellowship today it is because of tomorrow's need. Help us to go back to ordinary tasks to do simple things in a redeeming way, to perform common responsibilities with an uncommon spirit, and to face a disordered world with triumphant souls.

Eternal Spirit, by whom the humble are enlightened and the righteous are guided in judgment, grant unto us the grace of penitence and contrition, the gift of hospitality to thy leading and of obedience to thy will; and endue us with the faith that conquers fear and the courage that surmounts disaster. We acknowledge our common guilt for the disorder that afflicts the world. We remember with remorse and sympathy the multitudes of the hungry and bereaved, thy children and our brethren, upon whom the heavy consequence of our joint sin has fallen. Open ways for us to serve them; shed light upon the path that leads to their redemption and to ours; teach us all by the severity of thy just and law-abiding punishments the insanity of war and the true conditions of a saving peace.

Thanks be to thee for thy human ministers of light and love who have acquainted us with incarnate goodness, so that our eyes have seen it and our lives have been redeemed by it. For homes where fidelity and good will have made life beautiful, for friends whom we have loved and known, and for friends unknown, by whose multiplied service and sacrifice across the ages a great heritage has come to us, we thank thee. Make us worthy of this high company of the world's servants and saviors.

O God, who hast built thy Church upon the foundation of the apostles and prophets, Jesus Christ himself being the chief cornerstone, save the community of thy people from cowardly surrender to the world, from rendering unto Caesar what belongs to thee, from forgetting the eternal Gospel amid the temporal pressures of our troubled days. For the unity of thy Church we pray, and for her fellowship across the embittered lines of race and nation; and to her growth in grace, her upbuilding in love, her enlargement in service, her increase in wisdom, faith, charity, and power, we dedicate our lives.

Touch our hearts in these days with a fresh spirit of generosity. Upon every agency that dispenses the gifts of those who have to the needs of those who lack, let thy benediction rest. Save us from selfishness. Soften our hard hearts; save us from mean excuses. May there be no portion of the world today that our good will can reach where our gifts do not make the lot of some easier to bear.

Come close to us in our personal troubles. Some are here who have lately laid their dead away and their hearts are sorrowful; there are anxieties of body, mind, and estate, that need the healing touch of thy hand; there are prayers for wisdom, certainty, spiritual stability, and power. There are souls here shaken by temptation, bewildered as to which way they ought to go, or so defeated that they feel no hope. There is strength here, thy gifts of intelligence and power waiting to be used in a generation that desperately needs them. According to our needs may the riches of thy grace in Christ descend on every one of us.

We ask it in his name. AMEN.

[21]

6

ETERNAL SPIRIT, from whom our spirits come and in whom is all our peace and power, we humbly worship thee. Thou dwellest in light unapproachable. Thou art to us like the sun at noonday, thy brilliance too bright for our eyes to gaze upon, yet known to us by the light and warmth that bless the earth. We believe in thee with our minds; make thyself real to us in our hearts and consciences. Grant us an hour of spiritual hospitality to the Highest, and send us forth refreshed, purified, and empowered.

Grant us the grace of gratitude. Have mercy upon any here who find it difficult to be thankful. For some of us have lately been bereaved and our hearts are heavy and depressed. And some are in ill circumstance, anxious about the morrow and knowing not what will befall us there. And some are sunk in shame over iniquity committed or planned, and are wondering why this should be a world where evil is so easy and righteousness so hard. And some of us are burdened, not for ourselves, but for others whom we love better than ourselves. How can we be thankful?

Grant that in this hour of worship we may rediscover the faith that overcomes the world, may recall the endless benedictions by which our lives have been enriched, until thanksgiving rises warmly within us. Quicken our memories concerning the homes that nourished us, the friends that have sustained us, the books that have inspired us. Refresh our recollections concerning the blessings of our civilization, bought and paid for by other toils and other tears than ours. Lead us, supremely, to the Christ through whom thou hast so radiantly shined upon us, and at the foot of his Cross we will be grateful.

Give us tranquillity. Beneath the too great stress of this busy world grant us serenity and steadfastness, that we may be like him who built his house on rock, and not on sand. Give us stability, that with calmer eyes we may look on the restlessness and vicissitudes of life and possess our souls in peace.

Give us courage, Lord, courage to be honest, unafraid, straightforward, truthful. Build in us the basic virtues without which it matters nothing that we erect graceful superstructures of aspiring piety. Let there be no crooked way in us, no guile upon our tongues. Make integrity of life and character our portion now and evermore.

Give us vision, Lord. Thou hast not made this earth that the children of evil should triumph here forever. Thou hast made it that thy will should be done here as in heaven. In days of industrial greed, racial strife, and threatened war grant us insight to see that better days may come. Let us not supinely think that violence shall curse the sons of men forever, or the poor forever lose their opportunity in the degrading depths of the city's slums. Give us vision.

For all sorts and conditions of men we pray. Wherever in hospitals or in homes of sickness, disease has stricken down our friends or those whose names are quite unknown to us, there let our hearts be. Wherever on the far frontiers of the world missionaries preach the Gospel, or in sincerity and truth thy ministers at home proclaim thy word of righteousness, there let our hearts be. Wherever lovers of children guide their early steps, or servants of the aged make more peaceable the last roadway toward the sunset, there let our hearts be. Wherever soldiers of the common good fight stalwart battles for a fairer day of decency and good will on earth, for them our petitions rise.

This is our supplication before thee: that Christ, with his steadfastness, his courage, his faith, his sympathy, his victorious power, should dwell in us.

Grant it, we beseech thee, for his name's sake. AMEN.

7

ETERNAL SPIRIT, Lord of all worlds and Father of our souls, we worship thee. Out of our littleness and partialness weave us into thy larger life. As men never understood this earth until they looked away from it to sun and stars, no more can we understand ourselves until we see ourselves in our relationships with thee. Lead us up from our low levels and out from our narrow boundaries, that we may escape from our obsession with ourselves and, loving and serving something greater than ourselves, find what we are in thee. Set us in the great backgrounds of our lives. Remind us of the families from which we came, the fathers and mothers who loved us, the better heritage of our nation's life in which we share, the seers who have seen for us, the prophets who have spoken to us, the martyrs who have died that we might live, that, so seeing, our lives may be lifted up and we be grateful.

Grant us a new vision of the causes we should serve—justice in a generation full of wrong, unselfishness in a time when many suffer, peace in a day of violence. Show us that though we be little yet we can stand for the greatest truths. As a wayside spring, and not the great lake only, represents water, as a candle is an ambassador of light even as the sun, so take us in our littleness and make us representatives of those things without which mankind cannot live.

Release us from narrowness into wide compassion and sympathy. We acknowledge our selfishness; we are meanly content when things go well with us. Yet we live in a time filled with destitution, when lives are broken, and hearts are heavy, and bitter barriers of prejudice and jealousy divide mankind. Grant unto thy servants so sincerely to worship thee without pretense and sham that across all lines of division our hearts may today perform an act of all-inclusive good will.

Give us victory over private prejudices and mean vindictiveness, O God, for we would take into our care every sort and condition of man.

If hearts are here to whom such calls come in vain because they are too sorely hurt themselves, we ask thy strength for them. Not for soft and easy lives do we pray, but for great resources. Some of us are struggling against powerful temptations. Some of us feel the burden of grief and anxiety too heavy to be borne. We ask for stability, for inward reserves of spiritual power, that while the outward man is decaying the inward man may be renewed day by day. So, in the worship of thy sanctuary, may serenity, stability, and peace come to thy people.

Send us out, we pray thee, to face this troubled, difficult, and often cruel world. May we know how to lay soothing hands upon places that are hurt, and for ourselves keep clearly in our vision all that is excellent and beautiful, lovely, and of a good report. Give us radiance. Make our faith contagious. Help us to make goodness attractive. May Christ's joy be ours, and his promise of abundant life be fulfilled in us. May we be among those who help bring humanity to its victory, when the Kingdom of God's righteousness shall come.

We ask it in the Spirit of Christ. AMEN.

8

ETERNAL GOD, high above all yet in all, from whom to be turned away is to fall, to whom to be turned is to rise, and in whom to abide is to stand fast forever, we worship thee.

Like mountains whose summits are clad in clouds, so is thy mystery to us. We thy children on this wandering island in the sky, a speck amid the vasts of space, look up to thee. O God, let us not be confounded by the empty spaces or affrighted by world beyond world unfathomable. As thou hast put us into a great universe, help us to see behind it and in it a great God and lift up our minds to say, like our fathers before us, "Before the mountains were brought forth, or ever thou hadst formed the earth and the world, even from everlasting to everlasting, thou art God."

Above all, we have come to thee that thou mightest make real to us the universe within. There lie our fortune and destiny, for there truth may walk in shining garments, and goodness grow glorious, and beauty be beautiful indeed. O thou who hast taught us through thy Son that the Kingdom of heaven is within us, make true, we beseech thee this day, that description of our lives.

Meet us in the secret places of our souls. Walk thou through the hidden rooms whence too often we have banished thee. Let all that is low and abominable, selfish, vindictive, and of a mean report be put from us. Cast it down, discard it, good Lord, and lift up whatever is excellent and beautiful, unselfish and of high repute.

Look upon the human needs gathered in thy sanctuary.

Some of us come to thee in trouble, and out of the depths we lift up our souls. O thou who canst take a day in winter and make it shine, do thou, in the wintry season of our souls give us an illumined hour, and send us forth with such blue skies above us that it may seem the harbinger of spring and the promise of a summer's victory.

Some of us come to thee in joy, fortunate in love, happy in our families, prosperous in our estate. O God, for every benediction that makes more tolerable the pilgrimage of human life, and at times fills our souls with rejoicing, we thank thee. Touch every happiness with sacredness. Melt it into unselfishness; translate it into service; let it not be clouded by pride; make it transparent so that thy Spirit can shine through it to human good.

Some of us are young and come up out of the gates of the dawn. O thou who hast put into our control this fresh soil of a youthful life, let us not so exhaust it by frivolity that when the autumn comes no harvest can grow.

And some of us are old. Long ago we sang our matins in the morning; now we are ready for our evensong. Comfort us, we pray thee, through the final days of our pilgrimage, and let us catch foregleams of the eternal through the open door.

Some of us are strong. We are concerned about good causes that mean weal to human life. In disinterested love of truth we give ourselves to science; we sincerely care for schools and homes and communities; we lift up our thoughts for the nation and pray for a day of international neighborhood. O God, put courage into our hearts, wisdom into our minds, strength into our arms. Let us not by any temporary failure be swayed. Give us a long look and a deep faith in the Kingdom of God that shall come on earth; and send us forth, we beseech thee, with the baptism of thy Spirit so to live and work that we shall help to leave behind us a fairer world in which thou canst rear thy human family.

We ask it in the Spirit of Jesus. AMEN.

9

ETERNAL SPIRIT, whom the heaven of heavens cannot contain, much less these temples which our hands have builded, but who dwellest in the humble and contrite heart, we worship thee. From the violence of the world and the turmoil and confusion of our busy lives we turn to thee for an hour of quiet thought, meditation, prayer. Let the roiled waters of our lives settle. After the rapids and waterfalls of another week, grant our spirits a tranquil pool, and then send us out in a fresh direction and on a better course.

Ah, Lord, the mystery of life is very deep; we cannot fathom it. The explanation of this vast and varied universe does not lie within the comprehension of our minds. Today we pray humbly for light enough to walk by. Grant us that! Lead us in paths of righteousness for thy name's sake. Give us the eyes of faith that can see the way despite life's mystery and the world's discordant noises.

To that end lift us above the immediate and set our lives in the wide horizons of abiding verities. Our eyes grow too accustomed to man's ugliness and sin, to the world's tumult and disorder. Today remind us of the goodness that is here, of the beauty that our eyes have seen in nature and in human life, of friendliness that has been visited upon us, love that has sustained us, character that has undergirded us, and of thy goodness that has been patient with us. Today put Christ in our remembrance and those strong and radiant lives who have followed in his steps. Awaken gratitude in the hearts of some of us who have forgotten to give thanks, and around the evil that depresses us throw great memories and wide hopes.

Recenter our lives around faith instead of fear. Thou seest the justification of our dread, but put faith in the center, that sole and only conqueror of fear, so that some of us who came in troubled with dark foreboding may go out with strong conviction renewed and faith restored, empowered to overcome.

Center our thought not around our strength but thine. Our strength is but little. Alone and unaided we cannot handle even our own lives well, nor can we pit ourselves against the vast evil of hostile circumstance. Only with thy power in us and through us can we be adequate. If we could be strengthened with might by thy Spirit in the inner man, then we should be strong indeed, using even the ills of life to create finer character and a better world. So come thou close to us, one by one, and minister to our deep need of thee.

We lay before thee with solemn intercession the sorry estate of our world today, its violence and uproar, its trust in force, its menace of war. Ah, Lord, when shall our eyes see settled peace again? When shall the morning be glad as the sun rises, and the evening peaceable? When shall the air be no more laden with threatened battle and death? Beyond our power to see the possibilities, we pray for peace, a just and honest peace, that will give the world a lasting hope of brotherhood.

Past all those inner barricades that we erect against thy coming do thou press, Spirit of the living God, to unlock the secret doors in each of us, that there may be found no wicked way in us. Comfort our sorrows. Strengthen us where we are weak. Steady our spirits. And send us forth from this place to walk more worthily of the high vocation wherewith we have been called in Christ. Especially help any who are in such dire need that we must pray for them because they cannot pray for themselves. Forgiveness, inner sustenance, courage in danger, serenity under strain, strength to do what we ought to do and to stand what we must endure—for such blessings we pray. So let thy refreshment fall in benediction on some spirits here and bring them power to overcome the world.

In the Spirit of Christ we pray. AMEN.

ETERNAL Spirit, grant us grace to worship thee in spirit and in truth. Thou hast so made us that the glory of our lives is not in things below us that we master, but in the Divine above us that masters us. We are elevated by our admirations; we are enriched by our reverence. Grant us an hour of such spiritual wealth, made aware of eternal realities, captured by a vision of the Christlike life, lifted out of our littleness by dedication to abiding values and to thine everlasting purpose.

Cleanse us from our evil—our ugly egotism, our indifferent apathy, our mean ambitions, our sinful lusts—that we may be ready for this transforming experience. Grant us honesty in confronting and confessing our sins, sincerity in making restitution where we have wronged others, humility in seeking thy forgiveness, and resolution by thy grace and help to amend our lives.

Thou seest us, a generation victorious over the hazards of war, but frustrated and confused by the problems of peace. From a dismaying world we come into thy sanctuary. Here we pray for an hour of spiritual insight that, with thankful hearts, we may see afresh the light which even this darkness has not been able to put out. For the heritage of the Christian Gospel, for all the saints who from their labors rest, for the noble succession of the seers and prophets, for Christ, thy Son, who hast given us a Kingdom that cannot be shaken, for living friends who renew our faith in goodness and beauty, integrity and love, and for thee, O God, because of whom our human life is not a drifting raft but a ship with a course, a compass, a captain, and a destination, we thank thee. Marshal within us in these momentous times such resources of the spirit that we may be able to withstand in the evil day, and having done all, to stand.

Minister to our intimate personal needs. Spirit of the living God, walk through this congregation now and be the help and comfort, the inspiration and sustenance of our souls. In temptation, in illness, in disappointment and depression, in defeat when we are tempted to give up and in success when we are tempted to be proud, O God, restore our souls. May we hear thy voice speaking to each of us, reassuring us, challenging us, summoning us to dedicated and victorious living.

Especially may thy summons be heard by some wavering and uncertain soul who, standing at the crossroads of right and wrong, of Christ and Antichrist, cannot make up his mind. O thou who hast given us this mysterious power of initiative and choice, set our souls on high things and in this dangerous generation when for ourselves and our civilization we must choose life or death, the blessing or the curse, grant us grace one by one, in scorn of consequence, to choose for our devotion things worth living for and, if need be, worth dying for.

For our nation we pray that it may not miss the true path amid the world's confusion. For all efforts to create an ordered and peaceful human family our petitions rise—for our own sakes, for our children's sakes, and for Christ's sake, that he may see fulfilled the faith and hope for which he died. And for thy Church Universal we pray. Bind up her dissevered fellowship; enlarge her thought, her sense of mission, and the outreach of her service, that she may so proclaim and practice the Gospel of thy Son that thy Kingdom may come and thy will be done on earth.

Hear now the unspoken prayers that rise in silence from the deeps of our hearts, and to those needs that can find no voice save for thine ear alone minister according to the riches of thy grace in Christ Jesus, our Lord. AMEN.

O GOD, from whom come all good things in man and nature, we would sensitively open our spirits to thee this hour. Thou art never far from any one of us, and yet in this pavilion of thy worship we would more intimately find thee and be found of thee. Infinity of grace and goodness, lift us up into a new faith in thee and a new vision of thee. For dark hours come when questions rise concerning thee and doubts throng in.

The beauty of nature, its symmetry and order, harmony and color—that we see. The virtues of human life on its noblest altitudes, integrity and honor, courage and good will —that we see. The achievements of man's mind and character, the truth that science seeks, the beauty that art creates, the goodness that high-minded manhood gains—that we see. The victories of righteousness, where light has risen out of darkness and love has proved stronger than hate—that we see.

O God, from whose great reservoir of goodness these streams flow, make us more certain about thee, until today we too shall say, "The Lord is the strength of my life; of whom shall I be afraid?"

In this faith lift us up into a new courage. Thou seest our daily need of fortitude and valor. Save us from soft optimism. Let not sentimentality beguile us. Save us from saying, Peace, peace, when there is no peace, and may we never try to heal deep diseases with easy words. Give us honesty to face hard facts and yet, with it all, give us courage, we beseech thee.

Thou seest with what varied needs thy children seek thy face. O thou who dost meet us in the solitariness of our own souls, with thy still, small voice deal with us one by one. If we have sinned, grant us the grace of sincere penitence and renunciation, and cleanse us with thy pardon. If we are in grief, comfort us with the steadfastness of thy strong foundations under us that the storm may not beat us down. If we are in anxiety, clarify our vision and direct our steps. Unsnarl some tangled life in this company, we beseech thee. If we are proud, humble us, and if we have been humiliated, lift us up; and, so girded, send us out to be soldiers of the common good.

Keep us from selfish living in a dangerous time that cannot survive its follies without public-mindedness. Grant that upon some life here thy hand of high commission may be laid this day. O God, in a time that cries for leadership, let leaders rise. Especially to some young man or woman, whose eyes, being fresh to the world, can see, and whose mind and heart, being sensitive to thine approach, can feel the need of this time and the way out, may thy commission come.

So bring order out of the chaos of our confused thinking and living. Amid practical problems very complicated, amid questions of right and wrong very confused, thy children cry for guidance. Let thy word be a lamp unto our feet and a light unto our path, and may some perplexed spirit who has sought thy sanctuary see plainly the right road for his feet to take.

Because thou hast brought order out of the confusion of our inner lives, fit us to be better servants of thine in bringing order to this bewildered world. For the wisdom, courage, and sympathy which mankind deeply needs we pray. Send us out empowered for ministry. Help us to bring sanity into the madness of this world. May the touch of Christ upon our spirits make us wise enough to make the world a little wiser. Strengthen us to bring new courage to those whose lives move near our own, an unconquerable faith that despite the bewilderments of this present time love can conquer hate, peace rise triumphant over war, justice prove more powerful than greed, and the kingdoms of this world become the Kingdom of our Lord and of his Christ.

So grant that as by many paths we have come to this place of prayer and by paths so various go forth that only thine all-seeing eye can trace our divergent ways, coming in need we may go in strength to the praise of the name of Christ. AMEN.

O Lord, our God, we thank thee for all thy revelations which in times past have been sacraments to our souls. Once more thou hast opened the gateway of another morning. Once more the mountains and hills break forth into singing, and the trees of the field clap their hands. Lift up our hearts to praise thee. Let nature speak to us not of herself only but of the eternal artist on whose palette all her colors have been mixed.

We thank thee for thy Church, that fellowship of the sons and daughters of the Spirit who, across the generations, have kept the great tradition of goodness and truth. Many have been their names, various their beliefs, but at the center of their souls shone a great light, and by it thou hast made all the world more beautiful. Join us to their company. We rejoice in the music through which they have praised thee and the books in which they have revealed thee and lifted the earth nearer to the Kingdom of righteousness. We rejoice in the lives that, in their inner purity and truth, have stood for thee in scorn of consequence. Lift us up to be members of their company. Thus we would turn from the sordidness of life, from its din and passion, from its hectic busyness and its superficiality, and find once more our confident resource, our security, tranquillity, our peace and our power, in thee.

Deepen our faith this day. Give us a new grasp upon things unseen and eternal. Save us from being slaves of our eyes and believing only what they see. Help us to understand that through the veil of the visible the meanings of life must come, invisible, eternal, spiritual.

Quicken our hopes this day. Save us from the current cynicism of our generation, from its skepticism and its disbelief in the possibilities of human life. Lift us above its derogatory and condemning attitude that would kill all things that are right and make impossible anything that is lovely. Heighten our hopes, and send us out believing once more that in the heart of humankind are possibilities which thy touch, O living God, can quicken into reality.

Expand our love this day. O God, transcend our selfishness. Help us to rise above our hatefulness, our vindictiveness, our prejudice, and our provinciality. If any of us have brought hate into this house today, may we find it flowing from us because thy love has been shed abroad in our hearts.

We beseech thee, our Father, for all hopeful and constructive movements now afoot in human life. We pray thee for all scientists seeking truth, for all teachers trying to guide the minds of the coming generation, for all physicians at their healing work, for all those who love beauty and seek to create it, for all philosophers who endeavor to cast light upon the deep problems and mysteries of human life, for all servants of the common good who in sincerity and truth are lifting this low-lying humankind of ours up to the kingdom of fraternity.

We lay before thee the deep, unspoken needs that have been brought into this sanctuary. Go thou into the hidden corners of our hearts. If unforgiven sins are there, grant us true penitence that thou mayest pardon them. If there are weaknesses there which, unknown to us, may yet cause our downfall, give us knowledge of them that we, being made strong where we are weak and given power where we are frail, may come off more than conquerors. So, not according to our merit, but according to the riches of thy good will and wisdom, minister to us this day in the deep places of our hearts.

We ask it in the name of Christ. AMEN.

13

Eternal Spirit, so high above us that we cannot comprehend thee, and yet so deep within us that we cannot escape thee, make thyself real to us now. In a shaken world we seek stability; in a noisy world we need inner peace; in a fearful world we want courage; and in a world of rising and falling empires we crave a vision of thine eternal Kingdom whose sun never sets.

Seek us out, every one, in the special circumstances and needs that each soul faces. Young and old we come, the merry-hearted and the bereaved, families together here and solitary souls lonely and far from home, some of us tempted to be proud of the world's prizes and some crestfallen because of failure, some strong in body and others striving to keep the inward man renewed while the outward man perishes. O Sun of our help and strength, be to us like the sun indeed and shine this morning into every window.

While thou dost comfort us, kindle also within us sincere penitence. Let some austere word of righteousness be spoken to our consciences today. Save us from our ignoble excuses, our cheap defenses, our unworthy self-deceits. Give us grace to be honest with ourselves, that we may rightly judge our dealing with the personality thou hast entrusted to us, with the friends and family that surround us, with the opportunities thou hast put before us, and with the stewardship committed to us.

We pray for the peace of the world. Stay the evil forces that withstand good will and lay the fuse which will explode another war. For wisdom to seek peace and pursue it, for faith and character to use aright the powers man has in his unworthy hands, we pray. To that end our intercessions rise for the United Nations, for all conferences seeking disarmament and peace, for our nation, its President and all who influence its policies, and for us, the whole body of the people, that we may prove worthy of the stewardship of opportunity entrusted to us.

With thankful, yet with burdened, hearts we pray for thy Church. Across the dividing lines of mankind's bitterness today keep her fellowship real and vital. Beat down, in thy mercy, the cruel iniquities that in many lands persecute her saints, deny her liberties, destroy her sanctuaries, and even refuse to her the training of the children of her own households. And here, where we have liberty, help us to maintain her strength, rear our children in her nurture, seek afresh to understand her Gospel, and make real to the ends of the earth the salvation that is in Jesus Christ, our Lord.

Make this church, we beseech thee, a loyal servant of thy cause. To the ministers, the laymen and laywomen of this congregation grant vision and dedication, wisdom, generosity, and devotion, that we here, a company of Christ's disciples, may exhibit his Spirit, further his work, and be faithful servants of his Kingdom.

Now may thy Spirit touch us all with some healing wisdom and strength. Kindle our faith, rebuke our infidelities, make sensitive our consciences, dedicate our strength, fortify us in our troubles, and send us out strong in the Lord and in the power of his might.

In the name of Christ we pray. AMEN.

ETERNAL GOD, before whom sinners cannot stand, we come humbly into thy presence. Out of the turbulence of the world, our hearts disquieted by its confusion, our lives contaminated by its sin, we come to thee. Give us an hour of insight and cleansing; grant us grace to be honest with ourselves, sensitive toward our neighbors, reverent toward thee.

We dare not come to worship thee without bringing our brother with us. Father of all men, who hast said that we cannot love thee unless we love our brother also, we would come bringing him with us in our hearts' compassion and good will. Before we seek forgiveness, help us to be forgiving; before we ask for mercy, help us to be merciful. Take from our hearts the hidden grudge, the secret vindictiveness, the lurking hate. Give us a catholic and inclusive spirit of sympathy and understanding. From all bigotry and prejudice of race and class deliver us. Teach us what it means to care even for those who despitefully use us, and so abiding in love may we abide in thee.

Though we come with our brother in our sympathy, nonetheless thou seest how alone we are. We come from the world, where men look on the outward appearance, to thee who dost look upon the heart. We ourselves hardly know the secret motives of our own lives; we are so busy in the world that we seldom meet ourselves face to face. O God, seek us out now in the inward, untrodden recesses of our souls. When we confront our severest troubles, our profoundest temptations, we are solitary, and when death comes we die alone. Companion of the companionless, inner source of strength, comfort, and fortitude, deep well from which the living waters rise, be with us today.

We bring before thee our anxious concern for the evils

of the world. We lift up all nations in our prayer, those whom we call enemies and those whom we call friends. Thou seest how swift and impetuous our judgments are; we condemn some, we wish well to others—how can we do otherwise? Yet here in thy sanctuary may we remember the vaster horizons and perspectives of thy grace. Thou seest the far-flung causes of our human tragedy; deep within us all thou knowest the sins that have caused it. Thou, who art no respecter of persons, carest for the victims of man's inhumanity among all peoples. Thou hatest tyranny and injustice; in thy purpose stand the welfare of all nations and the fraternity of mankind. Spirit of the Highest, keep us from hopelessness and disillusionment. Grant us the courage of our fathers who in desperate days were undismayed, and in the face of many adversaries did not lose their faith.

Draw close to any in special trouble here. Some are ill, or are burdened for their sick at home. Some have lately laid their dead away, and their hearts lie buried in the sepulcher. Some stand with their backs against the wall in desperate temptation, almost overwhelmed. Spirit of God, may thy saving grace come to some such souls today. And strength is here, talents unused, powers undedicated, by which thou couldst lift thy Church and thy world to a better day. Lay thy hand on the best in us and devote it to thy Kingdom's coming.

We pray in the Spirit of Christ. AMEN.

ETERNAL SPIRIT, from whom we come, to whom we belong, and in whose service is our peace, grant us today openhearted hospitality to thy presence. From the hurry and turmoil of the world we come to thy sanctuary to be quieted, cleansed, guided, and empowered. Forgive our sins, comfort our sorrows, allay our fears, challenge our consciences, and open our souls to thy victorious invasion.

Thanks be to thee for every revelation of thyself in nature's orderliness and beauty, for every evidence of thy presence in history, for every unveiling of thyself in triumphant souls, and for Christ over all. Thanks be to thee for thy self-revelation within our hearts, for days of clear shining when thy presence has been real, for days when the high tides have risen in our spirits and we have been confident of thy companionship!

With thankfulness we worship thee, but with contrition too. We do not enter thy sanctuary with clean hands or pure hearts. Give us honest eyes to see our faults. Here in thy presence we would search our ways, despise our unworthy excuses, hear the voice of conscience plainly speaking, and, forgiven for the past, we would go out to build stronger characters. Create in us a clean heart, O God, renew a right spirit within us.

We lift our earnest, anxious prayer for mankind's peace. For all the stricken, impoverished, homeless, hopeless peoples we intercede. Beyond our power to see the way, drive thou a road through these jungles and morasses that man's ill will and violence have wrought. Save us in this nation from pride of power, and from all self-complacency deliver us. So use the too small wisdom of our wisest leaders, and the too partial goodness of our best statesmanship that, nonetheless, our children, in a more decent world, may rise up to call this generation blessed.

Quicken in us by our worship all that is worthiest and best. Awaken the spirit of appreciation. If we have grown tired of life, burdened by its anxieties, ruffled by its perplexities, fatigued by its monotony until we ask of what account it is to live, awaken us from our disillusionment and unhappy brooding into the spirit of appreciation. Make vivid to us the blessings that surround our lives and have surrounded them since the day when first we were cradled in our mother's arms. Make clear to us the goodness of life, to which too often we grow blind, that out of low, discouraged moods we may be lifted by our worship to praise and thanksgiving.

We pray for thy Church, that it may be reformed again, born anew into largeness of spirit and seriousness of devotion, forsaking the mint, anise, and cummin for the weightier matters of the law, and ministering worthily to the need of this troubled generation for faith and courage, for good will and peace.

Now separate this worshiping congregation into its individual souls. Come to each of us, Spirit of the Highest, in our concern for those we love and in all our personal griefs and anxieties. If we are fortunate and proud, humble us; if we are stricken and humiliated, lift us up; if we are bereaved, comfort us; if we are tempted, succor us; if we are confused, direct and guide us. And send us out sure that nothing can happen to us that thou and we together cannot meet.

We pray in the Spirit of Christ. AMEN.

SPIRIT OF GOD, who inhabitest eternity but who dwellest also with him that is of an humble and contrite heart, make our spirits now thy sanctuary. Here in this outward temple, where we worship thee, say to each of us in secret, "Know ye not that ye are a temple of God, and that the Spirit of God dwelleth in you?" So make sacred our inner lives today; build altars there, and kindle the flame of praise, confession, dedication. In vain we worship thee in a church unless our souls are sanctuaries too, unless in the chancels of our hearts we pray.

In the light of our inward worship, give us grace to be honest with ourselves about our sins. Swift to see the mistakes of others, grant us vision to see our own, honestly to face them, deeply to hate them, courageously to turn from them, and by thy grace to be delivered from them. Grant that we may not today see the mote in our brother's eye, and miss the beam in our own.

In the light of our inward worship, help us to see beyond our sins and failures into our possibilities. Lift some downcast soul today out of the slough of despond about himself and his generation into fresh faith and hope. Come to some whipped and beaten spirits here with the gospel of thy transforming power, reminding them that not what they have been, not what they are, but what by thy grace they may become, is their life's true meaning. O thou Light that lighteth every man coming into the world, shine in us now that we may see ourselves as we might be at our best.

For all the dear and intimate concerns of our families and friends we pray. The hallowed names our public worship does not voice, thou hearest in the secret worship of our hearts —the children, the wives and husbands, the youths, the aged, the tempted, the sick. No man is the whole of himself, O Lord; his loved ones are the rest of him. For them we pray as for our own souls.

We pray for all our human race—strange passengers upon this wandering island in the sky. Because our life is so mysterious and this universe so great, we deeply need to be sure of thee, confident that universal power is in the hands of eternal goodness. Be thou to us this day the guide of our pilgrimage, and give us the peace of God, passing all understanding, that the world cannot give and cannot take away. Let us not lose faith in thine eternal purpose, despite the confusion and dismay of this troubled generation. Especially grant to our nation wisdom and sanity, courage and patience; may our leaders put the nation's and the world's welfare above party; and when our children's children remember us in times to come, may they be able to give thanks for our devotion to justice and liberty and peace.

Awaken in us the spirit of brotherliness. Enlarge our sympathies, soften our hard hearts. Save us from the crass materialism of this present generation; let not that enemy invade the holy of holies of our spirits and take its place upon thy throne. May Christ be born in us, driving out our unkindly prejudices, until across all lines of race and caste and color all mankind is brought within the scope of our respect and care, that we may call nothing that thou hast made common or unclean.

Now take our church and this worshiping company into thy care and keeping. There are hearts here made bitter by the ills of life, souls crushed by life's troubles, consciences discouraged by the power of life's temptations, and spirits endangered by the pride of worldly success. Minister to us all, not according to our ability to ask, but according to thine insight into our need and thine infinite resource in Christ. AMEN.

OUR GOD and Father, in whom we live, from whom in vain we try to flee, grant us in thy sanctuary now a saving experience of inner quiet, serenity, and peace. We have been restless and overbusy in a noisy, troubled world; we come to thee seeking spiritual stability and strength. Thou enduring foundation that no storms can shake, thou deep well that droughts cannot exhaust, thou inner citadel that no foe can seize, with needy lives we seek the resources of thy grace and power.

Deep in our hearts remind us of things we ought never to forget.

Recall to us our blessings, that we may be grateful. Loved ones who have passed into the world unseen; friends whose loyal affection supports our lives; the great heritage of the past, bought with the sacrifices of our sires; all the daily goodness that sustains us, the opportunities that beckon us, the resources of beauty and truth that enrich us; and Christ overall, blessed forever—recall to us such sources of spiritual wealth and power, that we may be thankful.

Remind us of our sins, that we may be penitent. Here where thy light falls in judgment on our lives, revealing the darkness in them, save us from unworthy excuses and evasions. Recall our ill tempers, our resentments and infidelities, our harmful tongues, our selfish pride, our hardened hearts, our neglect of opportunity, and our contentment with trivial living. So chasten us with sincere penitence, and lead us to amendment of life.

Remind us of the hope of the world, that we may not be overborne by its confusion and disaster. Lord God Omnipotent, the beginning and the ending, thou still art God; before thee no evil can permanently stand, and no lie finally triumph. The kingdoms of this world shall become the Kingdom of thy Christ, and men shall yet beat their swords into plough-shares and their spears into pruning hooks. Renew our faith in thee and thine eternal purpose, and let not our confidence or devotion fail because of the fury of the wicked, when they boast themselves in the day of their pride.

Recall to our remembrance the fellowship of thy Church. We acknowledge our unpayable indebtedness to the pioneers of our faith, and to the continuing company of thy true servants across the centuries. Thanks be to thee for thy Church. Purify and empower her now to meet the need of this challenging time. And in this congregation of thy disciples keep our fidelity true, our care for all sorts and conditions of people sincere, our own lives genuinely Christian and our service effectual.

Watch over this nation, we pray thee. Save us from the pitfalls of selfish pride and misused power. Guide our leaders that we may help mankind to find the paths of peace. And upon us, one by one, so let thy grace come that, facing our temptations, bearing our griefs, sustaining our anxieties, and rightly dedicating our powers, we may be true servants of thee, and of thy Christ.

In his name we lift our prayer.   AMEN.

ETERNAL GOD, out of the noisy world and the strife of tongues we come to this quiet place to worship thee. Far from us thou never art, but by the insensitiveness of our own hearts we keep thee distant. In this hour of opportunity grant us the grace of receptiveness that into responsive souls we may welcome thee.

Thou art Spirit and we would worship thee in spirit and in truth. By many intimations thou hast revealed to us thy reality and living presence—in radiant souls through whom thou hast shined upon us; in the order, beauty, and wonder of the world; in victories of light over darkness, of goodness over evil, of love over hate. Up these overflowing streams from thy fountainhead we press in this hour of worship to find thee, the fountainhead itself.

Often we have brought to thee our weaknesses: sins to be forgiven, fears to be allayed, anxieties to be overcome, discouragements to be driven out. Again today with our many wants we come to thee. Dry reservoirs, we need thy rain; discordant hearts, we need thy harmony; leafless trees, we need the renewal of thy springtime. But above all we pray that thou wilt not simply relieve our weakness, but wilt lay hold upon our strength.

We bring to thee our minds. Fallible they are, yet rightly used they could give dignity and meaning to our lives and service to mankind. God forgive us that we so misuse them! Spirit divine, with great work needing to be done in this world, lay hold upon some minds here today, that we may think more deeply, proclaim our faith in thee more intelligently, and work more wisely for the enrichment of mankind's life and the coming of thy Kingdom.

Lay hold upon our courage. We thank thee for the high

gift of daring. For all the bravery that human life exhibits we are grateful. Forgive our misuse of this noble power. Lay thy hand upon it. May we fight well the good fight for righteousness, for personal character, for social welfare, and for mankind's peace.

Lay hold upon our good will. Forgive us that we use brotherly love so narrowly and poorly. Extend its domain, we beseech thee. Enlarge its reach over the bitter boundaries that often hem it in. Let no mean prejudice in us hold it back. Grant us good will toward all sorts and conditions of men of every color, every nation, every creed.

Lay hold upon our faith, we pray. Faith can be the victory that overcomes the world, yet see how we put our faith in small, unworthy things. Lift our faith on high. May we believe afresh in thee, in the eternal purpose which thou didst purpose in Christ, in the infinite value of the human soul, and in thy coming Kingdom.

O God, so often we have come to thee, presenting our feebleness; today we come presenting such strength as is ours. Take it and use it as thy graving tool to carve thy will in this world. Cross the inner thresholds of our hearts. Comfort us in bereavement. Steady our spirits in sickness. Keep our hearts steadfast in practical distress. Let not the anxieties of this world overwhelm us. And, empowered by thy refreshing companionship, send us out to be soldiers of the common good.

We pray in the Spirit of Christ. AMEN.

19

Eternal Spirit, hope of the souls that seek thee, strength of the souls that find thee, we worship thee, praying for that inner refreshment and renewal which only thy presence can bring. Through another week the world has towered above us with its huge problems and has assailed us with its turbulence, and we have grown anxious, fearful, perplexed, inadequate. We need some shepherd to lead us in green pastures and beside the still waters, restoring our souls. Surprise us today with some unexpected gift of thy grace, some needed insight and guidance, some vision of new possibilities, some fresh resource of strength and courage. Let this visit to thy sanctuary be to some of us the beginning of a new era, as though once more at the burning bush thy voice said to us, "The place whereon thou standest is holy ground."

We pray thee for inner, spiritual victory over our lives. Grant us this triumph when we face hardship. We dare not ask to be spared life's difficulties and tragedies. Whatever strength of character we have achieved, whatever fortitude and patience we possess, has come from handling hardship. But we pray that we may rise above it, be superior to it, have power to transcend it, that we may build it into the fabric of our characters and weave it into the texture of our souls.

Grant us this victory when our lives are prosperous. Thou seest, Lord, how deeply we desire happiness and love it. For all that makes life joyful we thank thee. Help us, nevertheless not to be hurt by happiness, not to be enfeebled and made selfish by it. May we transcend it, and use it well, building with it more radiant and serviceable lives.

Grant us this inner victory as we face our daily work. We thank thee for tasks that give worth and meaning to our days. Despite the anxiety which it entails and the fatigue it brings upon us, blessed be God for work! Make us adequate for our responsibilities. May our sense of vocation be victorious over routine and monotony. We ask not for deliverance from our tasks nor for smaller burdens, but for sufficient strength to crown our daily work with unselfish usefulness.

Grant us victory, we pray thee, over our temptations. Have mercy upon us, for we are exceedingly beset by enticements to evil. May the good life, revealed in Christ, shine in our eyes today with an attractiveness that evil cannot have. Above all we pray that we may so handle ourselves that we may not hurt and harm others. Thou hast woven into our lives those whom we deeply love, so that whatever we do we do also to them. Help us to be our best for their sakes, and may we never by our weakness or infidelity injure and despoil them.

As thus we pray for ourselves, we pray for the world, and especially for all those who labor for mankind's good. For all physicians and nurses, caring for man's bodily ills; for teachers in our schools and colleges, training the minds of the the young; for social workers, relieving the distress of the unprivileged; for men and women in business and the professions who put the public good before private profit; for all statesmen working for honesty in government and peace among the nations—for these we pray and for thy Church. O God, make the Christian Church more Christian. May the Spirit of Jesus descend upon her and invade all who represent her, that the day of the Lord's victory may come at last.

In the Spirit of Christ we pray. AMEN.

20

ETERNAL GOD, deep beyond our understanding and high above our imagining, we worship thee. We thank thee that we cannot comprehend thee, for if thou couldst be caught in our nets, if we could run the lines of our weak thought around thy being and thy ways, then wert thou too small a God. We glory in thy greatness and thy depth beyond our comprehension.

Be to us, we beseech thee, what the souls of men across the centuries have sought to find in thee. Be to us a refuge. For the storms of life are heavy, the tempests beat upon our ships, and we need harborage and anchorage. Throw thy greatness around our littleness. Be to us the citadel of the eternal amid the anxieties of time, and let some hearts in this company rejoice that thou art our refuge and that underneath are the everlasting arms.

Be to us our judge. For when we compare ourselves with ourselves and with others, too easily self-complacency takes possession of us. Thou Spirit of all beauty, truth, and goodness, be thou our judge. Expect of us more than we expect of ourselves. Humble us with some fair vision of loveliness in character and in deed that will shame us from our self-contentment. Grant that some soul here may see thee high and lifted up, and in contrition amend his life.

Be thou to us a guide. For it is not in man that walketh to direct his steps. If thou hast no purpose, then are our purposes vain. If thou hast no plan, then is our building vain. If thou hast no will, then do our steps walk waywardly and know not where they go. We beseech thee that for the guerdon and reward of our worship light may fall upon some path, and some soul, confused amid the perplexities of life, may see the road that he should take.

Be to us a friend, not far off but close at hand, available for every day's most common need, so that we may but part the inward curtain of our souls and find thee there. O Eternal, so great and yet so close, make us aware of thine abiding presence and be to every one of us henceforth the inner Friend, the unseen Companion of our pilgrimage.

As thus we lift our petitions, spoken and unspoken, before thy mercy seat, we think of all souls, praying to thee around the world. Across all the lines of race and creed and nation, our sympathy goes out to them today. We are one brotherhood of man upon one planet. God forgive us that we have made of it so ill a place, when peace and brotherhood, justice and equity and good will might have had their habitation here. Shame us out of our waywardness and ill will, we beseech thee, and beginning with ourselves let us seek thee in Christ, that, as a fire spreads, so the contagion of Christ's Spirit may kindle all mankind.

Especially we beseech thee for some soul here hard bestead, his back to the wall, fighting some temptation, all but overthrown by anxiety of estate, grieving for the waywardness of those dearly loved, brokenhearted with bereavement at their death. Come thou, beyond our power to pray for them, close to all needy souls. We thank thee that we do not need to stay defeated; that we can be reborn, transformed, redeemed from defeat to victory. Grant that triumphant experience to some soul here today.

We ask it in the Spirit of Christ. AMEN.

21

ETERNAL GOD, high above our imaginations, whose judgments are a great deep, we worship thee. We seek thee in the sanctuary that we may be saved from ourselves. Small creatures are we, too much absorbed by trivial busyness, our lives, we confess, filled with temporal details. Today in the place of worship, in awe before thine eternity and greatness, we would gain altitude and horizon. Carry us out of ourselves into interests larger than ourselves. Let saints and scientists speak to us, the memories of history and the thoughts of seers, that, so seeing ourselves citizens of a great world, we may be greater because of it.

Save us from our weak self-pity. Our complaints rise before thee, as have the lamentations of our fathers before us. Dost thou not sit throned in light unapproachable? Canst thou understand how heavily life bears on us when the waves and the billows go over us? Yet save us from this, our self-pity. Give us deep resources of interior strength that we may face life with adequacy, may rise above the difficulties that confront us and carry off a victory in spite of them; that life may grow strong from within and be triumphant without; that we may rejoice and be glad in it, difficult though it is, and sing in thy house that we are more than conquerors through him that loved us.

Save us from weak excuses. Give us the honesty to face our sins. We acknowledge that we practice subterfuge and will not be candid concerning our failures. Grant that in this place of honest prayer, where thou art from whose eyes no life is hid, we may see the evils that we do harming not only ourselves but those who trust and love us. Let there be such sincere and moving penitence among this people that lives may be redirected, that evils may be cast aside, that hands may reach out to take hold on solid good, and that thy Kingdom may come the more, in our lives and through them, because we have worshiped here.

Save us from our narrow interests and cares. Help us to live out our lives in other lives. Knowing that there is no good that comes to each that should not come to all, and no good that may come to all that should not be the care of each, knowing that we are members of one brotherhood, help us when we pray to say, as the Master said, Our—Our Father, our debts, our trespasses, our daily bread. Help us to take the common needs of every day and lift them up into the great fellowship of the human family. Cast down prejudice and across all barriers that ancient days have built of race, creed, class, and nation grant that our generosity and friendliness may flow out to all the sons of men.

Especially we seek thy benediction upon any lives here overthrown in anxiety, fear, and sorrow. O God, in the quiet of our silent prayer may thy Spirit move among this people and upon stricken hearts lay a healing, cooling hand. Let the fever subside. Let serenity, tranquillity, steadiness, and peace come now into some life that sorely needs them. Throw the horizons of thy greatness around us and be our unseen Friend.

We ask it in the Spirit of the Christ. AMEN.

22

ETERNAL SPIRIT, who out of the mysterious womb of nature hast created us, spirits also, with minds to see truth, hearts to love beauty, and wills to choose righteousness, we worship thee. As fire ascending seeks the sun, so seek we our parent source. As rivers flowing into the sea are but the sea itself that has fallen in rain upon the mountains, so have we come from thee and go unto thee. O God, in whom we live and move and have our being, our source and goal, we worship thee.

We who through another week have sought the fulfillment of our ambitions in the world, now bring them to thee within the courts of thy sanctuary. We would see and test them in the light of thy countenance. Here we would have them arraigned and tried, sifted and purified.

We bring our doubts to thee. Let thy clear shining dissipate them. Make them like transient clouds that have drifted across our skies. Rise upon us, thou Sun of righteousness, and give us a radiant day in our souls.

We bring to thee our anxieties. We lay them before thee pleading that if possible our heavy burdens be taken from us, but, if not, answer thou our prayer that we have strength enough to bear them. Grant us a wide margin of reserve around our need, and strengthen us with might by thy Spirit in the inner man.

We bring to thee our sins. Some of them we hate and some of them we love too well. Lift us out of the low-lying levels of our ordinary days and grant us perspective around our sinning. Give us the insight to see the harm done to those we love. Help us to see how, though sin seem private, it holds back the forward march of thy Kingdom of righteousness upon the earth. Make lovable in our eyes the things that are lovely and hateful the things that we should hate.

As thus we plead for personal blessings, we remember also all sorts and conditions of men. Breathe into our hearts, Spirit of the living God, good will and generosity. May we gather up into our sincere intercession all the nations, creeds, and races of mankind. Break down our prejudice. Save us from unfraternal partisanships. Let pettiness die as thy love rises in our souls. May we care afresh what happens to mankind. So re-create our spirits into the likeness of thy Son that all this week we may be considerate, tolerant, generous, and kind.

We commit unto thy care our nation. For leaders who in days past thou hast raised up to be our guides, blessed be thy name! Make us worthy of the sacrifice that has been built into the foundations of the commonwealth. Save us from our own folly, and from all national idolatry that puts another god on thy throne. From unrighteousness and lawlessness, collapse of personal character and public integrity, good Lord, deliver us. Let pure religion, sound intelligence, and uprightness of life be the blessing of this people.

Now, grant to each of us thy peace. Still us from the too great noise and busyness of men. Let the sediment of our roiled spirits settle. Purify the stream of our life, run it through thy sunlight, and grant that from this place we may go forth with thyself more real, life more alluring, thy Spirit more present and powerful.

We ask it in the name of Jesus. AMEN.

23

ETERNAL SPIRIT, take our too easily perturbed spirits in thy calm hand today and breathe into them serenity and power. From the noisy foreground of our life, filled with anxiety and busyness, we turn to its background, the high hills from which our help comes. Give us elevation of mind and breadth of outlook and stability within, that we may return to life again reinforced and reassured. To this end help us to put out from our spirits those things that keep us from finding thee and keep thee from finding us.

We lay our sins before thee. Give us a hearty and moving shame because of them. The sins of passion, whereby the gusty storm we did not control hurt our own souls and our fellows; the sins of asperity and temper whereby with meanness of thought and unkindness of tongue we made days heavy for those who trusted us; the sins of ignorance, where, like those who crucified our Lord, we knew not what we did but by our awkwardness, our blundering, our stupidity, wounded other lives; the sins of social outlook and attitude, where we let the prejudice and selfish interest of our class shut us in until we failed to take all humanity into our sympathy and care. O God, clear from our hearts the sins that keep thee from finding us.

We lay our doubts before thee. For all honest doubt and sincere questioning, all acknowledgment of mystery beyond our power to apprehend, all unsatisfied curiosity that leads us on, thanks be to thee! These are thy servants to drive us out of our complacency, where we have dwelt too long, to seek adventures thou hast in store. But, Spirit of the living God, beneath these doubts give us still some footing for our lives, some stable faiths that this world's vicissitudes cannot shake, some strong assurances of things unseen and ever-lasting.

As thus we seek thy help for our own spirits in this troubled time, we pray for the troubled world itself. We acknowledge that mankind's tragic ills are no denial of thy presence but the affirmation of it. Thou art the God of judgment who hast set us in a moral order where no man and no nation can with impunity defy thy laws. O God of judgment, who speakest in the thunder as well as in the sunlight, speak still until thou hast persuaded us away from our social folly and sin. Yet encourage us also, in our deep need, by giving us in our day some victory of righteousness over iniquity, of justice over injustice, of brotherhood over ill will, of peace over war, that we may be strengthened again in our faith and hope. Send us out from this communion with thee and with our own souls, to be better citizens of the whole world and members of the brotherhood of man.

Now draw close to souls so sadly darkened that their prayers can hardly rise above the clouds of their own troubled days. Upon bereaved spirits lay thou the cooling, guiding, steadying hand of eternal hope. To anxious spirits bring interior sustenance, that, because they have been strengthened within, they may be able to handle circumstance without. O God, transfer the crux of destiny in some spirits here from the environment about them to the strength of their own souls within them. Give us triumphant spirits that all our lives may be changed, and victories may be won for our sakes, for the world's sake, and for thine. AMEN.

24

ETERNAL GOD, who art the hope of the ends of the earth, be our hope in this place of prayer. Lead us to the rock that is higher than we and be to us a high tower and a strong defense against the enemy. For our foes marshal their hosts and encompass our souls—our anxieties and fears, our sins and follies, our failures, humiliations, doubts. See how the enemies of our spiritual life beleaguer us. O God, put upon the lips of thy servants a new song this morning, "The Lord is my light and my salvation; whom shall I fear?"

Take the cloud from our vision that we may see. Give us insight to discern truth from untruth, the high from the low, the clean from the unclean, the enduring from the transient. Grant us horizon, perspective, and clarity of mind and spirit, that thy servants, bewildered and confused concerning the way they should take, may find the path made clear, thy word a lamp unto their feet.

Strengthen our faith. Save us from credulity and all superstitious acceptance of things unsound and untrue, but all the more give us a steadfast trust in those things worth man's believing, and a deep and steady faith in those truths in which a man, confiding, shall not be shaken.

As thus we pray for our own souls, our sympathies and prayers pass over all boundaries of race and creed and nation to every worshiping soul and praying assembly on the earth today. Whether in church or temple, mosque or synagogue, wherever thy people lift their thoughts to thee, O thou eternal God, greater than all our names for thee, larger than all our human symbols and imagining, do thou come down to bless. We confess our partialness. We pray thee that our neighbors of other creeds may confess theirs. Bind us together in a common humility and penitence before the one God and

Father of us all, and make our faith in thee no longer a cause of division but a unifying power to draw our human family together.

We lay upon the altar of our intercession this sorry, storm-tossed world. We remember the distress and catastrophe everywhere among the nations. Forgive us that we so have sinned against light, and that instead of founding a peaceful order of brotherhood under law, we have turned our backs upon the sunshine and have set our feet toward darkness and night. Ours is the sin, O God, the sin of all of us, that violence stalks broadcast across the earth. Bring the people to penitence and the rulers of the people to thy mercy seat, we beseech thee, that in the day of our opportunity we may choose light and not darkness, law and not slaughter, brotherhood and not enmity, peace and not war.

And now draw near to the stricken souls who hardly can pray for the ills of the world, because their own ills oppress them so heavily. Upon bereaved spirits send thine eternal comfort, to shaken souls thy power. Into tempted spirits send thy reinforcement for the day of their trial, into disappointed hearts new hope, into restless and strained minds thy peace that passeth all understanding, that the world cannot give and cannot take away.

We ask it in the Spirit of Christ.   AMEN.

25

ETERNAL GOD, our help in ages past, our hope for years to come, we worship thee. Strengthen our faith in thee. This world is not a child of chaos only and the offspring of chance. We believe in thee. But today we seek an experience deeper than belief. We would have the Divine real to us, O God, dominant in us, controlling us, comforting and stabilizing us. O Spirit of eternal God in whom we believe, make thyself real.

Our sins have been real to us; our passions and our prides —we have loved them. They have crowded into the center of our consciousness and to do their bidding we have spent our thought. O God, make our virtues real to us. We thank thee for the divine fire that burns somewhere in every human life. Brush thou the ashes and the cinders from that hidden flame and let it be rekindled in our hearts this day. Make virtue real to us. Unselfishness and generosity, decency and kindliness, whatever is worthy of praise and is of a good report, lift it up, we beseech thee, and make it real.

Our troubles have been real to us. We have broken out in violent complaint. We have been rebellious and have pitied ourselves. Our sorrows and bereavements, the ill fortunes of our practical estate, have occupied the center of our thought. O God, give us a new perspective. Make our blessings real to us. Help us once more to count the benedictions in the past that have made life worth the living, our friendships, the family ties dear and beautiful through which thou hast ministered to the comfort and the loveliness of life. All that the seers and prophets of our race have bequeathed to us, the spiritual traditions of a civilization bought and paid for by other tears and other sacrifices than our own—make our blessings real.

O God, who without our asking it hast called us into this strange pilgrimage of mortal life, our cowardice has been real to us. We have been afraid of life, conscious of inferiority, burdened by a bewildering sense of our moral inadequacy for living. Make our courage real. There are stout chords yet in our hearts. Strike them, strong finger of the Son of God, until they vibrate in us. Lift us out of our timidity and fearfulness into confidence, courage, and faith. Send us forth from thy sanctuary, girded once more with the armor of the living God, that we may be strong in our generation. We come of a soldier breed that have fought great battles unafraid and have fallen on sleep undishonored. Make us worthy of our heritage. Make our courage real.

O God, our selfishness has been real. We have nursed and coddled ourselves. Make our unselfishness real. Lift up the horizon of our imaginations to take in this whole world of need. We pray thee for the industrial life of this nation. Most prosperous among the peoples of the world, save us from falling on our own sword. Lift us up into magnanimity and generosity, into justice, into a Christlike care, intense and passionate, for what happens to the sons of men. Grant, we beseech thee, a new baptism of interest in the world-wide brotherhood of man. Let the forces of peace conquer the forces that make and that love war. Especially we beseech thee for thy benediction upon those who sit in conference concerning ways and means for bringing concord out of strife among the nations. Above, beneath, and round about the fallibility of human counsel, bring all their good efforts to a wise, victorious issue.

These things we ask because thou hast revealed thyself to us in Christ through whom thou hast come to us, through whom we come to thee. AMEN.

26

O GOD, who wast, and art, and art to come, before whose face the generations rise and pass away, we worship thee. Thou who hast made this universe so mysterious that what is infinitesimal is as marvelous as what is infinite, be thou as deep within us as thou art far above us. By the secret intimations of thy presence, by quickening of conscience, by the dear solicitude of love and friendship, by memories of sacred hours and hopes of possible futures, speak to us and make thyself real to us, Spirit of the Highest.

Gather us into the catholic and comprehending arms of thy mercy, O God, a various company of folk met beneath this hospitable roof—the young that they may have light upon their path, the mature that they may have strength for their daily burdens, the elderly that they may not lose the light of the eternal morning. Take us into thy personal consideration—the strong, that we may be dedicated, the weak, that we may be empowered, the proud, that we may be humbled, the humiliated, that we may be lifted up. Grant that we who came in dismayed may go out with fresh courage, the faithless with renewed trust, the fearful strengthened with might by thy Spirit in the inner man.

Keep us, we beseech thee, from confusion of mind and dismay of heart amid the turmoil of our present days. Why must the good causes of righteousness and brotherhood be so withstood by evil and our fairest hopes confront costly sacrifice and proud gainsayings? Lo, mankind has within its grasp the things that might make this earth beautiful and human life decent and brotherly. Forgive us for our sins, save us from our misuses of our powers, keep us strong in faith and unbroken in courage. Raise up leaders for the people and grant, we pray thee, that Antichrist may yet be put down and peace bless our family of nations.

To that end we pray for thy Church. Make her a truer representative of her Master. Make her more fit to be the conscience of the nation and the world. Grant thy special grace on all missionaries of thy Gospel, standing in difficult places, sometimes amid the wrath of devils and the scorn of men. Let thy benediction rest upon us here at home in places of privilege outwardly, but in places of challenging responsibility too, where we also have sinned against the brotherhood of man, and need penitence and cleansing. Empower thy Church that we may still stand guard over the great highways of love and peace and brotherhood, until from long detours mankind comes back to them again.

Come to us one by one to meet those inner needs where we face disaster of mind, body, or estate. Grant that we may turn even our adversity into a friend. Thanks be to thee for the Cross, for without the Cross there would have been no Christ. We confess before thee that if life were all smooth there would be no patience; were it all easy, no courage, no sacrifice, no fortitude, no depth of character. We acknowledge before thee that what is most admirable is the child of adversity and of courageous souls unafraid to face it. Grant us that grace, we beseech thee, which has made all character great, that we may, even by those things that withstand us, grow in grace and in the knowledge of our Lord and Savior, Jesus Christ. AMEN.

27

ETERNAL GOD, whose purpose and whose laws pervade this vast universe, and make of it one world, we worship thee. We too in our personal lives need the wholeness and harmony which thou alone canst bring. From our confused and random living we would turn to thee to have our souls unified and made whole. Against all that divides our lives, scatters them, and makes them futile with confusion we pray to thee this day. Unite our hearts to serve thy will with single-minded devotion.

Grant us purposefulness, we beseech thee. Forgive us for our aimless living, for all the scattered devotion of our lives to things that matter little or not at all. Help us to discover a purpose in life so worth the soul's dedication that all our existence shall be drawn together about a central loyalty.

Give us faith, O God, faith in values so beautiful and good that our lives will be drawn into unity by our vision and love of them. Save us from cynicism, from skepticism, from all those maladies of the mind and moods of the spirit that spoil our lives, and help us this day to see thy will for us, excellent and august, beautiful and elevated, that we may believe in it and so be unified.

Give us love, O Lord. Bestow upon us the fine gift of friendliness. Forgive us for the way we tear our lives apart with our angers and hatreds. Teach us once more, Spirit of the Christ, that when we hate we do ourselves more harm than we do our enemies. Draw us together into unity because thou plantest good will at the center of our lives.

As thus we pray for those forces that draw our lives together and against those evils that scatter them in careless living, so we pray for those powers that draw our societies together. God forgive us for the prejudices and hatreds whereby we have cut asunder our humanity and have made of what might have been an earthly paradise a hard and bitter place.

Especially we beseech thee for those forces that unite our nations, for every cause that works for good will and peace, for justice and a sound mind. Against all that divides us, against all that is hateful and provincial, against all policies of selfish isolation, against all grudges that cut like a sharp knife through the co-operations of humanity we pray thee, and we beseech thee that thy benediction may so rest upon those who plan for peace that our children may live in a more hopeful world than ours.

We pray thee for better understanding and co-operation between the world's religions. Teach us with ever deeper and more sympathetic insight to look below the surface into the hearts of all who worship God. Be thou this day with every Buddhist soul seeking to discover the Divine; with every Moslem heart sincerely trying to do God's will; with every Hebrew mind endeavoring to make real to this generation the high ideals of righteousness which his prophets proclaimed; and let thy benediction rest on all who call themselves Christians, of whatever name or sign. Beneath all our differences teach us our brotherhood. Beyond all our varieties teach us our common goal. And so bring together, we beseech thee, the spiritual forces that ought to make for peace, that religion, no longer dividing men, may unite them in the cause of humanity and thee.

In the Spirit of Christ we make our prayer. AMEN.

28

ETERNAL SPIRIT, whom we could not seek unless thou hadst first sought us, give us responsive hearts today. We cannot lift ourselves to any paradise of moral excellence where thou dost dwell. We cannot invade the light ineffable of any heaven that is thy habitation. Who by searching can find thee out? Unless thou dost come down the little stairways of our lives into the humble place where we abide, we shall miss thee. We pray not for a change in thee but in ourselves. Make us receptive to thy presence. Make us sensitive to all that is noblest in our own lives through which thou dost come to us. Make us attentive to the still, small voice by which thou dost speak to us. We have known our godlike hours. Give us for the reward of our worship this morning another hour of communion with thee, from which we shall go forth knowing that we have been in thy presence.

Speak to us through conscience. Let some authoritative word of righteousness come to some heart here that needs it. Startle us out of our complacency. Summon us to ideals that we have forgotten. Refresh within us the memory of knightly hours when we dedicated ourselves to things worth living and dying for. O Spirit of the living God challenge our consciences.

Speak to us through our ambitions. Shame us from low motives of greed and selfish acquisition. Help us to set our hearts once more on things above where Christ dwells. Lift us up to dream of nobler things for our world, of international brotherhood, of industrial life dedicated to the service of man and not of mammon, and send some young lives, we beseech thee, forth from this place of meditation and prayer to consecrate their strength to the building of the Kingdom of God.

Speak to us through our loyalties. We thank thee for our nobler devotions—for friendships, for family fidelity, and all the dear and sacred ties by which we are woven into the network of humanity. If we have been faithless forgive us. If we have been inconsiderate and selfish recover us. Dignify and hallow our nobler loyalties to home, to country, to the Kingdom, and to thee.

Speak to us through our sense of gratitude. If we have clouded the sky of our own lives and that of our fellows with our whimperings and complaints, have mercy upon us. Remind us once again of those gracious benedictions through which thou hast shined to make our lives lovely. Bow us down in humility and then lift us up, we beseech thee, with a fresh sense of our unpayable indebtedness.

Almighty God, because men and women like ourselves, out of their need of thee, everywhere pray to thee, lift up the whole level of man's moral life. Wherever in temple or mosque or synagogue or church any sincere soul seeks thee, do thou reach down and answer with thy help. Especially we pray thee to make Christianity more Christian. Baptize us with the Spirit of our Founder, touch us again with the contagion of his loveliness, send forth men and women into statesmanship to do there what Christ would have done, send them out into industry and into family life to be there what Christ would have been, that the whole world may be redeemed to fraternity and peace.

And in the vastness of the Kingdom's enterprise let no one of us be lost, O God! Say thou to each of us that we matter, that the way we handle our lives, dedicate our strength, control our desires, love our fellows, and live honestly with them and with thee, matters to thy Kingdom.

In the Spirit of Christ we pray. AMEN.

29

ETERNAL SPIRIT, thou fountain of all that is excellent and beautiful in human life, once more we turn to thee, unreplenished, needing thy renewal; weak, needing thy strength; fatigued, needing thy rest. We have tried to content ourselves with lesser things but thou hast set eternity within our hearts. We are restless until we rest in thee. Into thy sanctuary we come with praise upon our lips. Yet save us from the ancient sin of casting palm branches before thy Christ at the week's beginning and crucifying him before the week's end. Give us sincerity, we beseech thee. From the ungenuine lead us to the genuine, from the unreal to the real.

O God of grace, who art able to strengthen us with thy Spirit in the inner man, so deal with us this day that high business may be done for thy cause in our hearts, that we may go from this place of meditation and prayer to be more worthy of our high vocation as thy sons and daughters.

Play, we beseech thee, upon all the chords of our lives. We who so often have placed ourselves at the disposal of the world's fingers to play upon, would in this hour come before thee that thy Spirit might touch the strings of our hearts.

Play upon our gratitude. If we have held our complaints so close to our eyes that we have lost the far perspectives of thy favor, grant, we pray thee, for the reward of our worship, wide horizons in this morning hour. Remind us of the homes we came from, of the fathers and mothers who nourished us, of the better aspects of the civilization out of which we have come, of causes once defeated, now victorious, for which others shed their blood. Teach us once again that we are not our own, that we have been bought with a price, that we may go forth to make our lives part payment on an unpayable debt.

Play, we beseech thee, upon our nobler fears. O thou who

hast given us the power of foresight, teach us anew the lesson of the springtime, that whatsoever a man soweth, that shall he also reap. If there are lives or families here already treading the pathway of careless dalliance which, pleasant now, must find its end in the valley of death, awake in us, we beseech thee, a holy awe of this law-abiding universe that so inexorably moves from cause to consequence.

Play, we beseech thee, upon our loves. Awaken within us the spirit of friendship and kindliness. Save us from our vindictiveness, disillusionment, and cynicism. If some have wronged us, help us afresh to see how some have blessed us. Kindle again the fire of good will upon the hearthstone of our better selves. Let benevolence, largeheartedness, tolerance, and friendliness have possession of our souls.

Strike, also, we beseech thee, the sterner chords. Awaken our devotions. O God, we pray thee for work to do, good work, and strength to do it with. Send us out into this great generation where no man need waste his life, to find our tasks in the home, the church, the state, and in the world-wide fraternity of mankind, that because we have lived and thought and toiled this earth may be a more decent place for thee to raise thy children in.

So play upon us, Spirit of the living God. Let all our hearts awake to praise thy name and then may we go forth to serve thy cause.

We ask it in the name of Christ. AMEN.

30

ETERNAL GOD, whose sun gloriously renewed the morning, renew our hearts within us. For though the earth be filled with beauty, and the gifts of thy grace lie all around us, and the doors of opportunity open before us, yet shall we not have eyes to see, nor faith to believe, nor power to appropriate, if our hearts be not right. Create in us a clean heart, O God, and renew a right spirit within us.

We bring to thee our foreboding thoughts about the world, our sorrow at the wars that ravage the peoples, our fears and apprehensions for mankind. We dare not leave them out of our worship for they are here. Help us to lay them on the high altar, under the shadow of the Cross. For on Calvary love seemed conquered by hate, goodness by evil, and life by death. Lo! how thy victory came, so that still our Lord's name is adored by all thy children. Grant, that in these days we may keep our faith in thee, Lord God omnipotent, Determiner of destiny from everlasting to everlasting, in whose strong hands are the reins of all the earth. Give us eyes to see again thy horses and chariots of fire upon the mountains.

We bring to thee our benedictions. Thanks to thee for all that is lovely and excellent in our lives; for friendships and families; for the fidelity of strong character; for the deep resources of spiritual power that we have found in thee in the days of our need; for great books and great music; for the beauty of the natural world, and the laughter of little children, and the salvation that is in Christ. Teach our eyes to see more clearly the meaning of life, its abiding values, its prophecies of hope, and awaken in us in the sanctuary the song of gratitude and praise.

We bring before thee our sins, in shame and penitence. Ah, Lord, help us to defeat these demons that invade our lives!

They come as though from some nether hell to spoil our happiness, wreck our homes, disrupt our families, and make us moral burdens to ourselves and to the world. Give us strength to drive them out. Grant us an honest hour of self-dealing, that our eyes may grow ethically clear, our consciences be strengthened, and our resources replenished as we worship thee.

We pray for our schools, recalling with gratitude the long sacrifices from which, as from travail, they have come. We thank thee for all faithful teachers spending their lives creatively for the children's sakes. With affection and expectation we think of the boys and girls who come and go through the doors of our schools. Grant such insight, such quality of mind, such enlarged vision and sturdy character in those who teach and those who learn, that the world through our schools may achieve the moral and intellectual foundations on which a nobler society may be built.

Grant thy grace especially to any in deep sorrow here. If we have visited the grave and left, as it were, our very hearts within the sepulcher, we bring our uncompanioned loneliness to thee for thy sustenance and help. Teach thou us to feel not only thy presence, but the presence of those who have fallen on sleep, a great company of spiritual witnesses, that we may worship here today, not simply a fellowship of those who chance to be alive on earth, but as well the noble living and the noble dead. So in every deep and intimate need, in temptation, in sorrow, in the prosperity that leads to pride, in the disillusionment that leads to despair, may we find the strength of God, in the Spirit of Christ. AMEN.

31

ETERNAL GOD, our Father, we come to thy sanctuary to adore and worship thee. Thou art greater than all our thought of thee. Only a margin of thy ways can we understand. Deep beyond deep, thy mystery is too profound for our plummets to fathom. Yet not alone in thy greatness would we see thee this day. We would know thee inwardly, secretly, intimately. We long for a richer and more radiant life. We have not fulfilled our possibilities. We are but dwarfs of ourselves. We would lay hold on the rich heritage of the sons of God which thou hast left to us in Christ Jesus.

To this end quicken our appreciations, and enliven our responsiveness and receptivity. For we have walked callously amid experiences where others have grown wealthy in heart. Troubles that others have used for the redemption of character have left us in bitterness and rebellion. Lift us to a nobler appreciation of our lives this day. Forgive us that so often we take from the day's rich offerings only a few herbs and apples and, content with triviality, forget the sun, the moon, and the stars. Make us responsive to the Highest this day, that we may have an enriched life.

Forgive our sins. The windows of our souls are often so soiled that thy light cannot shine through, and sometimes we have deliberately shuttered them, drawn the curtains of iniquity over them, and so our sins have separated us from thee. We pray thee for forgiveness and for a better mind. Redeem the souls of thy people that sins to which we have clung, we today may hate. Tear thou them from thy throne within us and help us to worship only thee.

For the privilege of fellowship in worship, we thank thee. Often we have shut the door and prayed in secret to the Father who sees in secret, but today we come where two or three are gathered together. That we may touch shoulders in the companionship of prayer we thank thee. We are moved with the feeling of one another's needs. Our imaginations run out among this people gathered here to think of the troubles borne, the happiness enjoyed, the bereavements, the perplexities of mind, body, and estate, the temptations, the opportunities for service. Hear the unspoken prayers of this congregation.

Our imaginations run out far beyond this company to take in all sorts and conditions of men. We pray for all who approach thee by other roads than ours and think of thee in other terms. O God, who hast said all souls are thine, who sendest thy sunshine on the evil and the good and thy rain upon the just and the unjust, come down the channel of every sincere aspiration in human hearts this day, and lift humanity nearer to thyself.

Have mercy upon us who have found thee in Christ, as we beseech thee for his victory. Give him the victory in his Church, called by his name but often unworthy to bear it. Baptize thy Church with the Spirit of the Master. Enlarge it with his magnanimity, his breadth, his generosity. Deepen it with his love. Make thy Church more worthy of thyself.

And give Christ the victory in our own hearts. Empower us this day, inspire us, illumine us. Send us out so to live in his Spirit, to walk in his ways, to be mastered by his ideals, to find power where he found power in the deeps of prayer, that we, not only by what we say, but by what we are, may leave this world a fairer place in which thou mayest rear the family of mankind.

We ask it in the name of Christ. AMEN.

32

ALMIGHTY GOD, whose heights are higher than our thoughts can climb, whose depths are deeper than our plummets sound, we worship thee. We have dared by faith to believe in thy love revealed in Christ, but we would also stand in reverent awe before thy greatness. Eternal Power, from whom have come the shining spheres, we adore thee. Children of a transient day, filled with feverish activities, engaged anxiously upon little tasks, we come once more to stand in large horizons and to ask thee to throw great perspectives about our lives. Cool our heat. Calm our little storms. Around our restlessness let thy rest come.

We lift up our sins in the face of thy greatness and are ashamed of them. They are mean and small. O God, in this great universe, with the majestic marching of thine eternal purpose through our generation, how can we be so little with our vindictiveness, our selfishness, our unkindness, our pettiness, our sensuality, with our surrender to temper and passion? We would live greatly in a world so great and a generation so significant. We do repent before thee of our sins.

We would lift up our troubles before thy greatness and be comforted. O God, we find stability, not alone in thy love, but in thy power. We hold our griefs so close to our own eyes that they eclipse the whole world for us. Today we would step into the presence of the Everlasting. The stars are forever in our skies yet we see them only in the night. So in our troubles, grant us, we beseech thee, visions of great distances, so that we may be calmed by the God of peace.

As we thus pray for peace in our own lives, we pray thee for peace among the societies of men. Thy compassions are not bounded by the lines that we have drawn and the barriers that we have built. Up many a stairway, strange to us, the aspirations of mankind over all the earth seek justice and good will. Come down every one of them, thou God of grace, wherever sincerity is, and minister to mankind's peace. Especially bless the Church that is called by the name of thine only begotten Son. Make us worthy of our Founder. Lift us up into the graciousness and hospitality, the generosity and compassion of his Spirit. Make us weary of the trivialities that have cursed thy Church and controversies that have dissevered her.

Look down, we beseech thee, upon our schools and colleges, and upon the youths who study there. For the frankness and candor, the sincerity and fearlessness of the coming generation, we thank thee. We beseech thee that thou wilt minister through them to the leadership of the world. Save them from triviality in such a day as this. O God, listen to our cry for leadership. Thy people are often like sheep without a shepherd. We pray thee for guidance and for men and women from this new generation who will have courage, vision, intelligence, and fearlessness to lead the way into nobler days.

Look down upon our nation, we beseech thee. In these days when we are grateful for the manifold plenty and prosperity which has been bestowed upon our people, give us also a profound sense of obligation and responsibility. God save us from the perils of mishandled power.

O God, who art very great, it is thy glory that thou carest also for us one by one. Thou art like the sun. Thou dost swing the planets in their courses, but thou quickenest the smallest garden that our hands have planted. Thou art the Father. Thy family is very great, but it is not thy will that one of thy children should perish. So draw near, in this service, we pray thee, to each soul here, and minister to us according to the riches of thy grace in Christ. AMEN.

33

ETERNAL SPIRIT, in whom is our strength for this world, and our hope for that which is to come, we would worship thee with sincere and humble hearts. We find life's problems difficult, its temptations strong, and our own will and wisdom insufficient. We can no more save ourselves than we can save the earth from winter to springtime by our unaided powers. As we need the sun to bring back the flowers and the leaves, so our hearts need thee, thy forgiveness and cleansing, thy refreshing light, the resource of thy presence, and the guidance of thy continuing fellowship.

With grateful hearts we worship thee. For the wonders of nature, for the heritage of noble sires who left to us the wealth of great traditions, for homes that sustain us, friendships that refresh us, work that gives life meaning and purpose, and for all those secret visitations of the Divine whereby we are inwardly made strong, we thank thee. Save us from all self-pity, from vain complaining and idle lamentation of our lot. Thou hast given us resources adequate for our daily need. Help us to avail ourselves of them, and match us with the challenge of these troubled days.

Have mercy upon our stricken world. Thou art the God of moral law who makest the way of transgressors hard, so that all nations, false as we have been to thy truth, suffer catastrophe together. Be also to us now the God of new vision and fresh hope. Show us the way, not back into our old denials of human brotherhood, but forward into a better day of man's redemption. Keep our hearts still sanctuaries of calmness and good will, of wisdom and unembittered mercy, that even amid the passion of these disturbed days the saving forces may be preserved in us, by which a new world may at last be built.

Especially we pray for the youth of our generation, for the

homes they come from, the schools where they study, the churches where they share the heritage of Christian faith. Watch over and befriend them in all the influences that shape their lives, in their reading and their games, their friendships and their family loyalties, their inner companionship with thee, and their awakening devotion to great ideas and worthy causes. Make admirable men and women of them, strong within and serviceable to their fellows, and let none of them fail for lack of faith and character.

For all who carry heavy responsibilities in the nation we pray. Save us from misuse of our national power. Protect the liberties, which our fathers bequeathed to us. Strengthen the United Nations and all agencies that seek peace and pursue it. Within our borders and around the world ease the tensions caused by racial prejudice. And because thou must give such blessings, not so much to us as through us, we pray that Christ may be made real to us in our worship. May his Spirit lift us above the vindictiveness of the world and its loveless lack of charity, its prejudice and antipathy, its racial hatred and national malice. Bless our hearts with magnanimity and generosity, and a sincere care for all sorts and conditions of men.

We pray also for the Comforter that Jesus promised. In temptation empower us, in anxiety calm us, in weakness fortify us, in doubt guide us, in grief steady us, and at last in death be thou the opener of the door into the world invisible and eternal.

In the Spirit of Christ we pray. AMEN.

34

ETERNAL SPIRIT, whom we worship with reverent lips, but too often with insensitive hearts, grant us today a vital experience of thy saving presence. Be to us not alone a holy name reverently spoken, but a living Reality within our souls. Shine in us, like the sun returning after the rain. Clarify our thoughts, elevate our spirits, deepen our faith and courage, and send us out to lay fresh hold on life because thou has laid strong hold on us.

For all that makes life rich and beautiful we thank thee. With gratitude we remember our homes and the affection and loyalty of our families. Gratefully we think of our friends and of their comforting and sustaining fidelity. For great books, great music, great art we thank thee, and for all noble souls—Christ over all—who, despite man's evil, have sustained our faith in man's dignity and possibility. Especially today we are grateful for thy Church. Despite her failures she has been to us the guardian of the great tradition, the trustee of our spiritual heritage, the preserver of faiths and principles which man forgets at his salvation's peril. Thanks be to thee for the truths which she has kept for us across the centuries, which have been our hope and our redemption.

As thus with gratitude we bring our best into thy presence, so too with penitence we bring our worst. Thou seest us with our self-centeredness and ill temper, our jealousy and animosity, tempted by worldly pride and lust. Thou seest us surrendering to our fears, losing our faith, compromising with evil, letting the world's chaos and our private troubles make us victims instead of victors in the battle of life. Spirit of the living God, come to some distressed and beaten souls here and repeat again the miracle of thy grace that, being transformed by the renewing of our minds, we may go out to be more than conquerors.

Upon the altar of our intercession we lay our anxious concern for this storm-tossed world. We are burdened by the tumult and bloodthirstiness of the nations. Ours is the sin, O God, the sin of all of us, that violence stalks the earth. Before it is too late, we beseech thee, bring the people to penitence and the rulers of the people to wisdom, that in the day of our opportunity we may choose light not darkness, law not slaughter, brotherhood not enmity, peace and not war.

Especially we pray for our children. God forgive us that we of elder years hand on to the world's youth burdens so heavy and unsolved problems so difficult. For the intelligence and character of the oncoming generation we pray. Make them wiser and better than we have been. As science opens the doors on unimaginable vistas of adventure, let not mankind commit suicide for lack of wisdom, integrity, and good will. Raise up leaders among our young men and women who will show us the way. If it be thy will, lay thy hand on some youth here today, who may be the pioneer of a new era.

For this congregation of thy people we lift our heartfelt prayer. May we not fail thee! May we match our opportunity with our devotion, and rise to the occasion that invites our service to the community, the nation, and the world. So enlarge our vision, our generosity, and our dedication that we may deserve thine approval as good and faithful servants.

In the name and Spirit of Christ we make our prayer. AMEN.

35

ETERNAL GOD, Creator of the universe, Maker of our bodies, Father of our spirits, we bow in awe and reverence to worship thee.

We come to thee because we have minds that seek to understand the meaning of our existence. The mystery of life is too deep for our plummets to fathom; yet we cannot believe that the mystery has no explanation. We cannot think that life is a process without meaning, a creation without a creator, lacking purpose and destiny. Only when we find in thee the Power behind all, the Meaning running through all, the Purpose that shall crown all, do our thoughts find rest. This day, O God, we would love thee with all our minds.

We come to thee because we are workers. We are concerned for our homes, our churches, our nation, and the welfare of mankind. We devote our lives to tasks in which we earnestly believe. We cannot think that they mean nothing and will issue in no worthy consequence. In hope we must be saved, and only when we turn to thee, saying like thy Son, our Lord, "My father is working still, and I am working," do we find strength and courage, confidence and power in our labor.

We come to thee because we are sinners. Sinners we confess ourselves to be, tempted by the prizes that evil promises but cannot give and, though often deceived, returning again to wrongdoing in search of happiness. We need forgiveness, and we need thy redeeming power. Our strength is not sufficient. We turn to thee who canst pardon us, and then canst strengthen us with might by thy Spirit in the inner man.

We come to thee because we are sufferers. Hardship has dug its ploughshare deep into some souls here. We need vision to understand and patience to endure life's tragedies. We need power not only to bear but to use our hardships, to build them into stronger character, and to come off more than conquerors. Because without thee we are undone with dismay or embittered with rebellion, we come to thee, thou God of all comfort.

We come to thee because we are lovers. Friendship binds us one to another and makes life beautiful. We rejoice before thee, grateful for our friendships and our families, unable to believe that love which so ennobles life is but an accident, revealing nothing deep in the heart of the Eternal. O God, thou art love. Teach our lips to say that once again and our souls to believe it, here in thy sanctuary.

We come to thee because we are mortals, whose years on earth are few, and who need a strong faith that shall make us unafraid of death. To know thee the only true God, and Jesus Christ whom thou hast sent—this is eternal life. May we here and now enter into it, and inwardly possess it, and being thus assured that death is an open door, may we both live and die with joy and hope.

So lift us above the too ordinary level of our mediocre days. May we find life's significance and satsifaction, its harmony and peace, upon those upper altitudes where thou dost dwell.

O God of the silent places, who hearest our most secret thoughts and dost understand our hidden wants beyond our power to pray, do for us what we most deeply need.

We pray in the name and Spirit of Christ.   AMEN.

36

ETERNAL GOD, who dwellest in the high and lofty place, yet also in him who is of an humble and a contrite heart, be to us this hour a living Presence. Be like the sun which, though it is far away, is with us in its warmth and light; like the air which though it encompasses the planet, yet is about us and within us with its vital ministries.

We come to thee because we desire liberated lives. Free us from inner tyrannies that imprison us. Deliver us from our fears. Haunted by dread and enfeebled by timidity, we make our own souls jails and our own anxieties jailers. Grant us fresh faith and new courage. Send us out with restored confidence in ourselves, our fellow men, and thee.

Free us from our doubts and disheartenments. This universe and our lives within it are mysterious beyond our comprehension. Let not the mystery frighten or dismay us. Quicken in us confidence that, even when we do not know the explanation, there is an explanation. Drive out our fearful doubts with a fresh faith. May we rejoice in the truth we can see and live by the truth that we do know.

Free us from our sins. We have often defeated thy purpose in our lives, have wronged our own souls and have hurt our fellows. We could have been transparent to thy shining, so that through us this world would have been a fairer place and the faces of our friends more radiant. Grant us that this day our consciences may deal honestly with us and that we may deal honestly with them. Send us out chastened, penitent, forgiven.

O God, free us from the imprisonment of our griefs. Let not sorrow master us. Give us altitude and strength of character that we may rise above life's hardships and be victors over them. Spirit of the Master, who didst make better use of thy Cross than of any other instrument life shaped for thy hand, give us thy faith and courage, that with the very hardships which beset us we too may help to save the world.

See how in the hands of our intercession we lift before thee the dear and sacred interests of our lives! We name our children before thee. O God, they are written on our hearts. We take counsel with thee concerning our homes. Grant that if any seed of bitterness is there it may be uprooted in this hour of prayer. We take counsel with thee concerning our city and our nation. Grant unto us a rebirth of holy indignation against things evil and corrupt. Baptize us with the patriotism of our sires who cared for the land of their love and gave themselves to it. Make us servants of peace, humaneness, justice, and good will, and, because we have cared and labored, may there arise here a more decent commonwealth better fitted for the family of God.

O God, lay thy dedicating hand upon some potential leader of thy people in this congregation. Call some life here to be thy spokesman, and may he answer, "Here am I, send me." See how our world plunges on its bewildered way, longing for wise guidance and not finding it. Have mercy on us who, in the midst of our strife and violence, face opportunities for world-wide brotherhood but ever turn our faces toward mutual destruction. Strengthen all minds that plan for disarmament and peace. Grant us wisdom that we may find the way out of our darkness into thy light.

So in church and state, in the United States and all the world, and in our own souls also, come to our help, and bring in the Kingdom of thy Son, our Savior, Jesus Christ.

In his name we pray. AMEN.

37

ETERNAL GOD, who without our asking it hast set us in this mysterious scheme of circumstance, widely we would open the doors and windows of our souls to thee. We crave the experience of thy people who have so felt thy nearness that they have cried, Whither shall we flee from thy presence? Whither shall we go from thy Spirit? In the beauty of nature, in the revealing relationships of friendship and family, in all that is excellent and worthy, courageous and full of hope in human life, in victories of light over darkness, love over hate, good over evil, become thou real to us and in the silence of our souls speak to us quietly that we may be sure of thy presence.

Through another week we have been tempted to be careless and ungrateful. Like streams flowing through our common days, goodness has been richly given and we have been thoughtless of the fountain. O God, today we thankfully acknowledge thee as the friend behind all friendship, the spring of all beauty, the source of all goodness.

Save us from dishonesty and every crooked way as we worship here. Let us not come before thee in court garments to appear as we think thou wouldst like to see us. Let us stand before thee as we are. If today our spirits are full of rebellion, make us candid with thee. Let us bring our lamentations and resentments into thy presence and speak them out frankly before thy face, complaining that life has not been just to us and that we have been ill treated. But, O God, help us to stay long enough in thy presence for thy healing hand to be laid upon us. Like storm-tossed seas when the wind goes down, growing quiet, so bring thou us to peace.

If we stand before thee with sins in our lives for which we are not penitent but which we dearly love, help us to be frank with thee. Save us from the futility of pretending penitence when we have it not. Grant us the grace of honesty to stand before thee, saying, O God, behold! What thou hatest we love. Nevertheless, give us grace to stay long enough in thy presence for thee to throw thy light upon the loveliness of Christlike living until we are drawn to that. Let not Satan beguile us by fashioning himself as an angel of light.

We come with our need for courage. Thou living Spirit, walk through this congregation and lay thy hand on men and women outwardly placid and comfortable, inwardly dismayed and beaten. For life has laid a heavy weight on some of us; death has come into our households; we have been disappointed in our friends; discouragements have met us in our practical affairs and some of us are torn by anxiety. O God we need the spirit of our fighting sires, who revealed the splendor of their souls when days were difficult. Speak to us, saying, Be not afraid.

Send us forth to be builders of a better world. Our hearts are burdened in this place of privilege and beauty by the poverty that afflicts the sons of men. Thy Providence has been sufficient and the world brings forth abundantly so that all should be fed, but our injustice and our niggardliness have made some rich and many poor. O God, have mercy on us who live in comfort lest we should be selfish in our privilege. Teach us not only to be merciful in overflowing charity, but to be just also that we may build a society in which such inequity may be impossible. Open our eyes that we may see; unstop our ears that we may hear the cries of those that call for help. Make our hearts sensitive and our consciences quick. Forbid that we should be among the cursed who stand at ease in Zion and care not for the affliction of Joseph.

In the Spirit of Christ we lift our prayer. AMEN.

38

ETERNAL GOD, our Father, wellspring of all that is excellent and beautiful, we worship thee. Through another week our eyes have looked too much on things below. We have watched too much the instruments of life, saying to some, Go, and they go, and to others, Come, and they come. Once more as thy day arrives we understand afresh that the glory of our life is not in the things that serve us but in the One whom we serve.

Grant us a fresh awareness of thy presence that we may repent. Stand us against the white background of thy purpose for our lives that we may be stirred from our too easy complacency about ourselves. Let not the vision crush us, but let it humble us. May we grow modest and ashamed in thy presence because we have cherished grudges and embittered life with vindictiveness; we have been blind to our duty when we might have seen it; we have been ungentle and unkind. O Spirit of Christ, make thyself real to this people that souls here sincerely penitent may find thy pardon and thy peace.

Grant us this vision of thyself that we may be rededicated to thy service. Going out into the common walks of life may we shed a new light upon the tasks of ordinary days.

If we are men of business may we glorify our calling. Forgive us that we have often dishonored it, that we have often made it unfair, bitterly competitive when it might have been fraternally co-operative. Help us to lift it up. Send out into the business world of this generation men and women who shall think highly of their vocation and make industry more just and humane.

If we are men of healing, help us to glorify our calling. Upon all physicians and nurses, all hospitals and asylums where those suffering malady of mind or body are gathered today, send thou thy benediction. Walk among the beds of sickness, thou great physician, helping those who must die that they may die well, and those who may recover that with a deeper significance visible in their lives, as though they had been saved for service, they may go out to live again.

If we are men of law, baptize us with a deeper apprehension of the sacredness of our task. Send us out into the law, we beseech thee, men and women who will live above the technicalities of their craft and love justice with a pure heart and a steady mind.

If we teach the young, let no carelessness on our part cause any one of them to stumble. Make us builders of personality, that in our day because of our faithful labors the world may not lack height of character, breadth of mind, and strength of leadership.

If we are men of religion, forgive us that so often we have dishonored thee and been false to the ideals of Christ. Whoever stands in a pulpit, bless thou his spirit today and touch his lips with a coal from off the altar that he may speak thine everlasting Gospel, carrying thy truth far into the hearts and consciences of those who hear.

If we are folk whose center is the home, help us to elevate the dignity of our high vocation. God bless all husbands and wives, all parents and children, all brothers and sisters here. In these intimate, dear, and deep relationships of our lives, help us to be true to one another and to thee.

So gather us up, we pray thee, according to our various occupations, and our deep and serious needs, into thine everlasting arms. Comfort those that mourn; steady those that stumble; walk with those that are lonely; companion those that are in deep distress; strengthen those that are weak; and send us down from this place of meditation and of prayer to live radiant and victorious lives.

We ask it in the name of Christ. AMEN.

39

ETERNAL GOD, our Father, we draw near once more in awe and reverence to worship thee. Often have we besought thee to fall upon us like showers of rain. Today we beseech thee that we may retreat into the secret places of our own hearts and find thee rising there like a spring, close at hand, cleansing and refreshing. Thou art the fountain of spiritual life within us. Thou art the source of every secret aspiration, thou art in everything that lifts and liberates our souls, and as thus we come to thee in worship we pray for genuineness and sincerity. Lead from the unreal to the real.

Lead us from the unreality of this world we live in, from the tinsel of the things we touch, from its shallowness and superficiality, from all that is cheap, showy, and ostentatious in ourselves and in our fellows. Make us genuine today.

Let our faith be real. We do not ask thee to give us faith. Thou seest how much of it we have, with what carelessness and credulity we bestow it on many passing whims. Lift up our faith, we beseech thee, that it may turn toward the Eternal. Set it on things above, where Christ is. Help us to believe this day in the Highest.

Let our love turn toward the real, we beseech thee. We do not pray to thee that we might have love. Thou seest that as the skies are made for winds to blow in so our hearts are made for love. Thou seest with what carelessness our affection turns everywhither and attaches itself to all manner of things. Help us this day to love the Highest when we see it.

Turn our hopes, we beseech thee, to aims that are real. Thou knowest the expectations that throng our hearts this day, the hopes that walk up and down the avenues and alleyways of our souls. Set our hopes on things that are genuine and right. Help us to serve with our hope and devotion the will of God in our generation before we fall on sleep.

As thus we pray for our own spiritual needs, we remember the numberless souls around the world, of many diverse faiths, who this day are seeking thee. Help us not to think of ourselves as though we uniquely were children of the light and they children of darkness. God forgive us for our pride and our condescension. We, too, are often children of darkness. Therefore we gather up all mankind in our supplication, and beseech thee for thy benediction on every soul sincerely seeking to do justly, to love mercy, and to walk humbly with his God.

We pray thee for all manner of Christians, of whatever name or sign, who have found in Christ the revelation of thee. Make us more worthy of our high calling. May thy Son break through the barricades that we too often have built against him. O God, draw all those who call themselves Christians to Christ and make us his better disciples, we beseech thee.

Draw closer together in amity and good will all classes and races of men. Forgive us that we so stress the distinctions that separate us here on earth. O thou who hast made of one blood all men that dwell upon the face of the earth, lift us to a higher plane this day, that race and nation may be seen as thou seest. Break down our prejudices. Give us generosity, magnanimity, kindliness, comprehensiveness of care. Make us citizens of thy universe.

Grant us thy spiritual resources that we may be more than conquerors over our private sins and intimate sorrows. May we transcend them, be superior to them, rise above them, so that today, going forth from this place, we may live, as never before, as becomes those who have had this high dignity bestowed upon them that they should be called children of God.

We ask it in the name of thy Son, our elder brother. AMEN.

40

ETERNAL SPIRIT, who from everlasting to everlasting art God, we worship thee. Receive us, proud men and women, too often content with our lives; strip us of our pride and stand us in awe and wonder before thee. Set us in the immeasurable vistas of this universe where thou hast housed us; confront us with the unfathomable mysteries of life; show us the questions we cannot answer, the problems we cannot solve, the achievements too great for our unaided strength; humble us that thou mayest lift us up.

Deepen our worship, we beseech thee, with the spirit of gratitude. Forgive us that ever we think of ourselves as self-made. Say to us, "What hast thou that thou didst not receive?" Make real to us our benefactions and our benefactors. Bring vividly before our imagination the personalities through whom thou hast shined to make our lives beautiful. Recall to us our homes, our churches, our friends, the great traditions of the race, the saviors, prophets, and seers of mankind, and Christ over all, and beget in us a humble spirit of gratitude.

Deepen our worship with the spirit of penitence. Save us from ignoble self-complacency. Startle us out of our self-deceit by some arresting vision of thy purpose for us in Christ. Give us the grace of repentance, the humility that asks forgiveness, the power to make restitution, that here there may be cleansing of life and rededication of spirit.

Deepen our worship, we pray thee, with some act of decision. Shame us that we ourselves are part of the world's problem and not part of its solution. Renew our minds one by one that each of us may present the world with one life, honest, sincere, dedicated, unselfish. Because of that may some friendship be sweeter, some home lovelier, some lives happier as the reward of our worship.

We present to thee our solicitude for our nation. In this day of need, when blundering stupidity so often puts all things awry, raise up among us men and women who know what our nation ought to do. Grant unto all of us the grace to rise above our individual self-interests, above prejudice of class and race, to a large and catholic care for the whole body of the commonwealth and all the people within it. Beat down the swords that are lifted against the peace of the world. Give thy people grace to make peace that will endure, and to that end raise up in the Church of Christ a fresh vision of Christ himself. Save us from our divisions! Let Christ say in his Church that the message may be heard in the world: "Blessed are the peacemakers: for they shall be called the children of God."

O God, save us from small and narrow thoughts of thee. Through countless channels thou dost seek our lives. Through many a door thou wouldst come in, if we would welcome thee. Though men deny thee, if they find truth they have seen thee. Though men disbelieve thee, if they love beauty they have met thee. Though men refuse our creeds, yet if they achieve goodness they have known thee. Today we would hospitably open our souls to thee. Spirit of God, descend upon our hearts.

Come close to lives specially burdened, faced with adversity in circumstance, with the loss of those whom they have loved better than themselves, with temptations too powerful for their unaided strength, with fear and anxiety that they alone cannot allay. Give us an hour of vision, hope, fortitude, and faith, in the Spirit of Christ. AMEN.

41

ETERNAL SPIRIT, far above us and yet deep within us, we worship thee. The world is too much with us. We are distracted by its varying claims and tossed by its many winds. We would escape for a while from its clamorous noises into another and higher world where there are unity and purpose, sense and meaning, faith and hope. Clarify our minds, we beseech thee. Give us great ideas that we may strike our roots into them and be strong when the heavy winds descend. Clarify our hearts. Save us from the folly of vindictiveness to the wisdom of magnanimity, and let good will have its way in our lives. Clarify our wills, we beseech thee. Save us from our cross-purposes and contradictory ambitions, and let some soul cry today, This one thing I do!

As we pray for ourselves, we know ourselves at one with all the souls of men. It is when we stand before the Eternal that we see of how little moment are the divisions of race and color, nation and speech, that separate man from man. Our souls are one; our deep needs are alike; our highest aspirations are the same. Thou hast made of one blood all mankind to dwell upon the face of the earth. Grant us not only to believe this but to live it. Make every one of us a faithful servant of human brotherhood.

We lift our prayer today for those who forget to pray for themselves. If there are boys and girls offering no petition for themselves, happy with the passing days, making no earnest supplication for their lives, we pray for them. Our hope is in them. Couldest thou, O Lord, lay thine hand on one of them, he might swing the gate of a new era for mankind. We lift up in our solicitous petition the youth of the world.

If there are churches that forget to pray for themselves, complacent and content, we pray for them. Thou didst give unto us so great a Founder, forgive us that we are so little worthy of him. Shame us in his presence. Impress his portrait on our imaginations that we may not forget him, that he may rebuke us constantly and then guide us toward that day when Christianity shall possess the quality of Christ.

We pray for all governors of nations, for all who hold significant office and position among the sons of men, if they are not praying for themselves. Forgive them for the ineptitude and selfishness with which the world is governed, and forgive us, the people, that we support them in it. Grant unto the leaders of the nations wisdom and insight, unselfishness and courage, lest they bring down the temple of mankind about our ears.

Especially we pray for those so harassed by difficulty and so lost to all high and vivid faith that they cannot pray for themselves. Grant to some such today a vision of blue sky through the gathering clouds that they may be sure again that the sun is shining. Give us radiance instead of darkness; give us stability instead of bewilderment; and set some sore-stricken and shaken soul today upon such deep foundations that his house shall not fall.

Now send us all out to make goodness attractive. Give us grace and radiance. May we make righteousness lovable because of what we are. Forgive us that we should ever misrepresent Christ, that the world should not see him in us. Lift us up until our religion shall sing in our lives.

We ask it in the Spirit of the Master. AMEN.

42

ETERNAL SPIRIT, thou dwellest in light unapproachable, beyond the power of our thought to comprehend or our imagination to portray. Yet thou art revealed to us in the order of the world we live in, in the truth our minds discover, in the inward presence of thy Spirit, and above all in Christ, thy Son. With reverent hearts we worship thee.

We would bring our fragmentary lives into the presence of thy wholeness. We would bring our transient thoughts into the light of thine eternity. We would bring our restless spirits into the calm strength of thine everlasting purpose.

See what complaints we have brought into thy sanctuary against the circumstances that have fretted us, against the human friends who have failed us, against the enemies who have wronged us, and even against the justice of thine order that has hurt us. Teach us, nevertheless, we beseech thee, to search our own lives, to see that each man is his own destiny, that each soul is its own heaven and its own hell. Send us back into our own souls to find there by thy grace, peace and power, and adequacy to conquer life. May we be victors and not victims.

O God, we would escape from ourselves this hour, from our little and partial selves, from our mean and selfish selves. We would escape from our fragmentary and broken selves into thy greatness. Teach us once again the everlasting mystery that only as we lose ourselves in something higher than ourselves can we find ourselves.

To this end give us a great faith to live by. From doubt and disillusionment, from cynicism and rebellion, deliver us, good Lord. For uncertainty give us confidence. Though we may not see all things clearly, let us see some great things plainly that we may live by them. O God, give us light enough to walk by.

Give us wisdom to live by, we beseech thee. We who walk so often blindly through the tortuous labyrinth of life, give us a clue this day. Let us have vision to see the way we ought to take through some perplexing circumstance. Let high decisions be made on the right side of great questions in thy sanctuary.

Give us love to live by, we pray thee. Enlarge our sympathies; deepen our understandings and compassions. Save us from resentfulness. Cast down within us pettiness and meanness, and lift us up to largeness of mind and heart that we may have the grace to take within the compass of our care those whom by prejudice we have shut out or through dislike have hurt.

Give us great causes to live for. O God, we thank thee for this difficult and serious time, this generation of many dangers and many open doors. Save us from living on a small scale in a great age. Open the eyes of some youths here to causes worth giving life to, that they may be glorified, not alone by what they are, but by what they identify themselves with. Lift us up into better days in the nation. Build justice into our economic order. Grant vision and courage to our statesmen. Make us equal to our international responsibilities and opportunities. And grant that we all may play a part in the things that matter most in our time, so that we may leave this world a fairer home for thy family.

We ask it in the Spirit of the Master. AMEN.

43

ETERNAL SPIRIT, thy servants seek thee not so much to secure what they desire as to open their hearts to the gifts which thou desirest to bestow. Through another week we have imposed imperious wishes on the world to get our will and we confess before thee the evil and unwisdom of our craving. Give thou to us not what we would ask but what thou wouldst bestow.

We seek easy and fortunate circumstance while thou hast in thine hand courage with which to face ill fortune and win a shining victory against hardship and adversity. Lord, give thy gifts to us—thy will, not ours, be done—courage, let it be, that we may prove ourselves the sons of God and heirs with Christ in overcoming the world.

We seek from thee happiness and like children would stand with open hands to receive life's pleasures, while thou hast a task to give us which will call us out of ourselves and claim all that we are for thee. A task, then, let it be, O God, according to thy wisdom! Give us a duty which will dignify our days that we may join the honorable company of thy true servants who, called of God, have found their vocation and have done it well. We would seek thy sanctuary, not to present our unwise wishes, but to put ourselves at thy disposal. Release thy power in us. Reveal thy wisdom through us, and grant that in and for and because of us thy will may be done.

We pray for the release of thy power not only through our single souls but through our families. Thanks be to thee for the home and for all the spirits across the centuries who by fidelity and high affection have built its fine traditions! Grant that through the families of this church thy will, purpose, and love may shine, and upon our children let thy benedictions rest. Make our homes strong schools of character and radiant centers of joy, and there may Christ never be shamed or forgotten.

Release thyself into the world through thy Church, O God. We confess her sins but we lift up before thee her opportunity. In a day when outward things absorb man's thought and spiritual life is so needy, let thy Church find again the authority of her message, the necessity of her Gospel, and the supremacy of her Christ.

We pray for those who are discouraged, cast down by evil circumstance, humiliated by moral failure, disheartened by the sorry estate of man's public life. Deliver us from the morass of our pessimism. Gird us with the fortitude of our sires, who in other days bravely stood their ground and trusted what thou couldst do with a minority. And we pray for those who are not discouraged, who do not care enough to be disheartened, for the meanly optimistic and the overly content. Arouse such to see upon what sorry days man has fallen. Deepen our care. Change us from complacent ease to dedicated work.

Cast down every barrier that shuts us from our fellow men. Make us one with all mankind, children of one Father, begotten of one God, living in one planetary home, destined to one common goal. Across the lines of race, class, nation, and creed our prayer goes out. Lift out of its degradation our humanity, blind to the things which belong to its peace, yet still bearing the image of God and the promise of an eternal hope. From our personal sins and our social inequities lead us to integrity of life and the righteousness in which alone is hope. O God, salvation is from thee and from none other. We open our hearts to thee. We put our lives into thy hands. We would be channels for thy grace, instruments for thy good will to use. Thy will, not ours, be done! AMEN.

44

ETERNAL FATHER, thy children, who have wandered far from thee, return once more to stand in reverence before thy face. From the superficiality of life, where so much that we see is cheap and so much that we touch is tinsel, we return once more to find in thee stability and depth and strength. From our lack of resource to meet the difficulties that besiege us and the temptations that assail us, we return to thee to find resource, reserve, and power. From the restlessness of life, its feverish haste and hectic ways, we return to thee to feel around our restlessness thy rest. From the harshness of life, its unkind ways and ungentle thoughts, from the vindictiveness of men and the harbored grudges that often make our own hearts bitter, we come to thee again to learn good will.

O God, welcome us, we beseech thee, granting us the priceless treasure of thy Spirit's presence. May souls that have been sore buffeted, that have fallen on discouragement and have lost hope, find power and comfort, fortitude and peace in thy sanctuary!

Make this day a sacrament of memory. Bring to our minds those recollections that shall cleanse and encourage, inspire and empower our hearts. We remember our homes. For the rich heritage that has come from them to us, for the sustaining traditions handed down from faithful homes to faithful sons and daughters, for the nurture and admonition of the Lord that we discovered in the tireless love of our families, we bless thy name.

We remember before thee those whom the world calls dead but who are not dead but alive. Bring them close about us on this day of reminiscence. Let those that have walked with us in times past be real to us that we may be inspired by the companionship of the world unseen and eternal.

We thank thee for the memories of our churches. For their faults and failures we seek thy pardon, but for all the grace and goodness in them, for the ways they have channeled to our hearts faith in Christ and love of Christlike values, blessed be thy name. Give us vision and dedication in our day to be more worthy of the saints and apostles, the prophets and martyrs who have borne a good witness to the Gospel, and have served their generation according to thy will before they fell on sleep.

We thank thee for our national heritage. For all that is unworthy there, for our selfishness, our pride of wealth, our vanity in prosperity, our forgetfulness that righteousness and liberty must be paid for by sacrifice in every generation, forgive us, O Lord. In these days when evil hands soil the sacred things for which our fathers died, when righteousness is forgotten in high places, when crime betrays the nation and the moral level of our living sinks, forgive us, good Lord. But for all that is noble and right, for all that is excellent and of good report, for contributions made to freedom, to democracy, to righteousness, blessed be thy name.

O God, our Father, who, amid all the vast concerns of the universe and of the nations, never dost forget the individual, cross thou the inner thresholds of our hearts this day. Thou knowest the anxieties there. Sickness is in our homes and we are solicitous as we remember before thee those whom we love better than we love ourselves. Temptations are in our hearts because of which we are burdened before thee. We face problems that perplex us, tasks for which we feel unequal. Our inner lives are battlefields where faith and fear, confidence and doubt, contend for the victory. We see within our lives failures that only thy mercy can pardon, and possibilities of good that only thy grace can bring to fulfillment. See thou the unspoken prayers which no tongue can utter for this varied congregation. Upon every secret aspiration send thy help. For every need send thy supply.

We ask it in the name of Christ. AMEN.

45

ETERNAL GOD, who without our asking it hast set us in this strange scheme of circumstance, guide us in the same, we beseech thee, that we fail not ourselves, our fellows, or thee. Teach us to look upon our life as a high trust. Remind us of the great souls of the past through whom thou hast shined gloriously to make the face of this earth more beautiful, the saints, apostles, and martyrs, servants of the common good, whom thou hast given to mankind. May we see them committing to our charge the stewardship of their high calling and saying to us, Life is a trust.

To this end teach us to see more vividly the faces of our friends, the loved ones in our family circle who have cared for us as they cared not for themselves, and all true spirits who have given us their affection and confidence. Let them say to us today, Life is a trust.

To this end make real to us the sacrifices of the past, the martyrdoms where with vicarious outpouring of life the world was uplifted, and those simpler, humbler services of heavy cost that plain men and women have contributed to make this earth more decent for thy human family. As thus we stand before the universal Cross, may it say to us, Life is a trust.

Especially to this end may we see today the Christ of God. Thanks be to thee for him! For the loveliness of his childhood, the beauty of his home, the integrity of his youth, for the greatness of his teaching, the grandeur of his life, the courage of his Cross, his glorious victory, and for his undying, undefeated influence, thanks be to thee! As he passes to us the high heritage of his memory, let his voice say to us, Life is a trust.

We pray for our families. No lovely thing has ever come to

earth save as behind it was a lovely home. Hast thou not called thyself Father and us sons and in our mutual relations called us brothers? Since we cannot understand thee except in family terms, God keep us from despoiling the family. Let thy benediction rest upon our households. Let no root of misunderstanding spring up among us. Let our homes grow beautiful that in their beauty we may see the likeness of thy Fatherhood and our sonship.

We pray thee for our nation and for our international life. So long ago the Prince of Peace was born with songs of good will to men, and so long tarries the fulfillment of the vision. Thanks be to thee for every hope that peace may come on earth! O God, help us to pray for peace so earnestly that to peace we may be daily dedicated. For the United Nations we intercede, for all who sit in conference concerning the world's critical affairs, for all who fight against hatred, bigotry, and violence in race relationships. Let our eyes see some triumphs of justice, and our hearts be inspired by the dawn of a better day.

We present to thee our personal lives. There are spirits here hard bestead by evil circumstance, crushed by bereavement, undone by anxiety, overwhelmed by temptation. O God, let some faith and hope and love come to the help of every worshiper.

We ask it in the name of Christ. AMEN.

46

ETERNAL SPIRIT, with reverence and humility we worship thee. Mysterious is this universe into which thou hast ushered us. We stand in awe before power beyond our thought to measure, distances that stagger our imaginations, questions that we cannot answer, and problems that we cannot solve. Mysterious is our life within us, that from the freshness of its springtime passes to the cold of its December. It is not in us who walk to guide our steps, O God. Lift us up, we beseech thee, that once more for our guidance and protection we may have an hour of insight and illumination, when the intuition of things divine and beautiful is real to us, and all that is august and excellent rises like the morning sun upon our path.

Lift us up, we beseech thee, from ingratitude to thankfulness. Strangely commingled is our life of things good and evil, happy and unhappy. Various and inconstant are our fortunes here. Forgive our eyes their tendency to center on the dark and troublous things. Forgive our imaginations that they fashion our lives into anxiety and gloom and absorb us in fears and forebodings. Grant us an hour of saner perspective and truer horizon. Let memory be our sacrament. Rekindle within us the fires of thankfulness. Remind us of homes where beauty dwells, of children that rejoice our hearts, of friendships that bless us, and traditions from times past for which others have shed tears and paid the price of sacrifice. Tune our spirits once more to gratitude.

Lift us up, we beseech thee, from cowardice to courage. Save us from self-pity. Recover us from our complaints. Lo! we are the sons and daughters of soldiers who fought a good fight before they fell on sleep, and were not afraid. Let us not betray the breed from which we come. Build into us also stout hearts that we in our generation may stand undaunted by fear, unconquered by adversity, untainted by cowardice.

Lift us up, we pray thee, from vindictiveness to good will. Let memories of the Savior steal upon our imaginations. If we are harboring grudges, if hatefulness has taken hold on our spirits, save us, we pray thee, from such a desecration of this holy hour. Bring sympathy back to us and understanding and the fair grace to put ourselves in others' places before we judge them. Lift us up above malice and evil speaking and unkindness of heart. Arouse in us his Spirit, who could pray upon the Cross for those who put him there. O God, help us to be Christians in our hearts because love is there.

Lift us up, we pray thee, from selfishness to service. Remind us of downcast and stricken lives. Let our imaginations run out into our prisons, the houses where the poor lie down in cold and penury, the asylums where disordered minds beat themselves out against their vain imaginings, the unprivileged areas of our city's life and of the world where blessings that we take for granted are little known, and hunger stalks and fear haunts and tomorrow is frightening. Wake up within us our forgotten kindliness. May multitudes be happier because, praying for this, we have gone forth to put our prayers into deeds.

And with all this, Spirit of the eternal Christ, lift us up from doubt to faith. Lift us out of our cynicism, our skepticism, our unwillingness to believe that the good may be true, into a courageous faith and certitude concerning God and his purposes. Illumine us, thou Sun of the morning, until not only shall our mountain peaks shine with a new confidence, but the very valleys shall feel thy noontime's splendor and we have faith again in ourselves, in our fellows, and in thee.

We pray in the Spirit of Christ. AMEN.

47

ETERNAL GOD, who art the hope of the ends of the earth, we worship thee. Thou art very great. The heaven of heavens cannot contain thee, much less these temples which our hands have builded. As high as the heaven is above the earth, so are thy thoughts higher than our thoughts and thy ways than our ways. May we not belittle thee by our worship, but do thou enlarge us.

Enlarge our thoughts. Thou hast set us in so great a universe, deep and high beyond our comprehension and imagining, that we would have our lives touched to greatness because we are its citizens. Enlarge our horizons. Expand our minds. Greaten our hopes. Withdraw us from the small and mean limitations of daily life, and as from some high hill give us in thy sanctuary large outlooks on thy world.

Enlarge our sympathies. From our small selfishness imprisoning us give us release today. Across the boundaries of prejudice and bitterness that color, class, race, and nation have built up, send out our understanding sympathy to take in all mankind. Are we not one family? Hath not one God begotten us? From the littleness with which our daily life is commonly afflicted, may we be emancipated in thy sanctuary. For freedom we cry, freedom from the limitations of our commonplaceness and their restricted sympathy, that we may perform here an act of compassion and care that will include all humanity. Touch us with pity for the common frailty of mankind. Teach us how much we need to be forgiven that we may find it easier to forgive. Save us from self-complacency and condescension, and may some service be rendered to the world by each of us, because we have worshiped here.

Enlarge our consciences, we beseech thee. We who have often repented of smaller sins that stain our ordinary days would now repent of large, collective sins by which we blacken the earth: our mutual iniquities that produce the slums of great cities, the injustice of penury in the face of plenty, and the horror of war where there might be brotherhood. Show us our share in these iniquities that make this earth a sordid place when it might be a home for thy family. Here in this place of worship before thee, whom nothing can content save righteousness, justice, and good will, may we repent.

See the near and dear interests which we would lay upon thine altar. O thou who settest the solitary in families, be with our homes. Save us from broken households and from spoiling the stability of family life around our growing children. If there is any root of bitterness springing up in any family here, O God of mercy, pluck it out and let love return again. For homes and schools and churches, the builders of character in our people, we pray thee.

Our private and intimate needs we lay upon thine altar. Not with the spoken word but with the unspoken petitions of our hearts we plead for ourselves and for those whom we dearly love. See how hard bestead and heavily burdened are some lives here. We need fresh resources of power by which to rise above our ills and win a spiritual victory. Canst thou not see here souls so distraught that they would willingly take their own lives away? O God, who art not afar off but lovest the habitation of a humble and contrite heart, come close to the spirits of thy people now, and give us deep interior reserves of strength, that we may transcend life, transmute it into good, and be more than conquerors through Christ that loved us. AMEN.

48

ETERNAL SPIRIT, not far from any one of us, in whom we live and move and have our being, we worship thee. In the world from which we come we often forget thee, and things visible, tangible, sensual so obsess our thought, fill our eyes, and preoccupy our hearing that we lose sight and audience of thee. O God, make real to us in the sanctuary the things that are real. Here let small things seem small, and great things great. Rearrange, we beseech thee, the perspective of our life. Round our little days throw such horizons that the seen and temporal may take their lower place, and the unseen and eternal capture our imagination and our faith.

We do not come to urge on thee our small requests, but rather to put our lives at thy disposal that thou mayest do in and through and for us what thou dost wish. Thou are great and we are small; thou art eternal and our lives are bounded by a sleep; we are thy servants; thou, from everlasting to everlasting, art the God of all. Take us in thy keeping. Mold us to thy will. Make us the instruments and implements of thy purpose. Release thy power, O God, through us into the world, that because we have met here some great thing may be done on earth, not by us but through us by thee.

Dost thou not desire our inward peace? Therefore put us, we beseech thee, in such relationship with thee that peace may come. Let the anxieties and fearfulness of ordinary days grow dim. Let the great affirmations of Christian conviction and faith be real in our hearts. Blow trumpets in our souls this day. Grant such margin of spiritual reserve around our need that the peace of God which passeth all understanding may be ours.

Dost thou not desire for us health of heart and mind and body? Therefore take from us those false anxieties, those needless tensions, which spoil our days, distract our lives, and make even our bodies ill. O God, the great and eternal God, who, when the doors are open, wilt come in to a man and sup with him and he with thee, so enter into our lives today.

Dost thou not desire for us righteousness? Therefore grant us honesty with ourselves that we may not evade our sins but, sincerely facing them, be deeply penitent. Especially help us to remember before thee those things whereby our ill doing has hurt not only our own souls but the lives of others. Because we cannot keep within the narrow boundaries of our experience the consequences of our wrongdoing, because our sins always flow over to destroy other lives, make us penitent, that with hospitable hearts we may welcome thee like the sun to drive out our darkness with thy light.

Dost thou not desire our joy? Our goodness can commend itself to men only when it sings, when it is radiant, resilient, and joyful. Thou who hast taught us that the fruits of the spirit are love, joy, peace, we would be to thee like channels through which thy springs of joy can flow today. So help us to handle our benedictions, remembering them with gratitude, and our troubles, surmounting them with victory, that our lives, being strong, may be glad.

And as thus for ourselves we pray, we think of all thou dost desire to do for the world at large. Across the boundaries of race and nation, over the prejudices that sever folk from folk, thy purposes run, planetary, all-inclusive, for the brotherhood of man. This is thy purpose. As we pray for it may we open up our lives to it that through us it may come to pass.

We ask it in the Spirit of Christ. AMEN.

49

ETERNAL GOD, Father of mercies and God of all comfort, we lift our hearts to thee in prayer and praise. From things that can be outwardly seen and touched we turn to thee who must be inwardly felt and spiritually known. Strange is this world where thou hast put us, full of questions hard to answer and evils difficult to understand, but full also of thy grace and goodness. For beauty in nature and art, for nobility of character and loveliness in family life, for fathers and mothers who have gone before and children who come after, for the rich heritage bought by the sacrifices of the past, we thank thee. Above all for Christ, whom not having seen we love, on whom, though now we see him not yet believing, we rejoice with joy unspeakable and full of glory, we thank thee.

Here in thy sanctuary lift up unhappy souls into joy, we pray thee, uninspired souls into illumination, crushed souls into fresh encouragement, defeated souls into moral victory, and enable us bravely to meet life and death, to fight the good fight, to keep the faith, and to finish the race.

From our worship here send us back into the world to be better Christians. Forgive us that we take upon our lips his name, who lived purely, believed deeply, adventured bravely, and triumphed victoriously, and yet are so false to his spirit. We remember with gratitude unutterable his sacrificial death that we might live. May we today with unveiled faces, beholding the glory of the Lord, be changed into his likeness. For Christlike integrity of character we pray, for his faith, his compassion, his indignation against sinful living and his unbounded love for sinners. Grant that we may be persuasive witnesses for the Gospel, because we live, yet not we, but Christ lives in us.

From our worship send us out to be better citizens of the

nation. Put depth and sacrificial meaning into our patriotism. May we not simply salute the nation's flag and sing its songs, but may each of us shoulder some burden of useful and redeeming service to our fatherland. We pray against the crime that curses our country, against the delinquency that afflicts many of our youth, against broken homes, impoverished slums, corruption in government, the misuse of power whether by owners of industry or organizers of labor, against the inequities that make a few rich and many poor. Help us to act as we pray. Enlist each of us in the ranks of those who serve their communities, who lift the level of our public life, whose love of country is translated into redeeming deeds. Make of our land a fairer place for our children after us.

From our worship here send us out to be better citizens of the world. O God, who so loved the world that thou didst send thy Son to save it, see our dismaying need of thy judgment and thy redemption, and have mercy on us. Save us from the despair that paralyzes action, from the apathy that will not undertake it, and from the faithlessness that surrenders to defeat. Seeing in our hands and hearts the evil that could cause mankind's destruction, may we also see the good that, by thy grace, could bring progress and prosperity, peace and brotherhood. Send us forth to build a better world, and if in our hearts there is any racial prejudice, mean ambition, cherished vindictiveness, that prevents the free flowing of thy grace through our lives to all mankind, O God, convict us and convert us, we pray in the Spirit of Christ. AMEN.

50

ETERNAL SPIRIT, who, whether we walk in green pastures, beside still waters, or through the valley of the shadow of death, canst be our guide and helper, we worship thee. Outwardly we bow with reverence in prayer, but thou seest how inwardly our disordered lives need thy guidance, our unclean hearts thy cleansing. From the contagion of the world, its low aims and evil practices, we come to thee to be transformed by the renewing of our minds.

If man's ill behavior has begotten resentfulness in us, so that we come to thy sanctuary with bitter and vindictive hearts, raise us to a nobler mood. Grant us good will and magnanimity that, thy love being shed abroad in our hearts through the Holy Spirit, we may remember how much we have been forgiven, and may be able to forgive those who have despitefully used us.

If the ill treatment, injustice, and hardship of the world have discouraged us, so that we come to thy temple with whipped and beaten spirits, O God let thy fingers touch some strong chords of courage in our hearts today. Set us on our feet again, revived and reinforced. Make men and women of us worthy of our sires, who in difficult circumstances have revealed the splendor of their spirits.

If our sins shame us, so that we come into thy presence with secrets in our souls which we would hide from our best friends, grant us thy forgiveness and restoration. There are hidden rooms in us, from the thought of which we shrink, and yet to which with fascinated imagination our inner footsteps ever more return. Grant us such repentance, such restitution to those whom we have wronged, such sincere desire for amendment, as shall restore us to thy favor and to our own self-respect. Blow through us, Spirit of God, till all our skies are clear again, and the sun shines once more.

If the world has been kind to us, granting us prosperity and peace, so that we come happily into thy sanctuary, grateful for many blessings, O God watch over us and guard our lives from pride and selfishness. May our blessings overflow from us to others. May our fortunate estate be made sacred by our devotion to our fellows and our service to our generation.

We bring to thee our anxious concern for the welfare of mankind. For the progress of science and the marvel of its discoveries and inventions we are grateful. But we pray thee for wisdom and character in ourselves and in our leaders lest, misusing the power that science has bestowed, we turn a blessing into a curse. Save man from committing suicide with the very instruments his hands have builded. Open our eyes to see that this new, proud generation needs humility and wisdom, Christlike good will and the spirit of the peacemakers, if we are not all to perish.

To this end grant to thy Church everywhere throughout the world a fresh sense of its divine mission. Save us from apathy. Save us from trivial concerns. Show us anew the dangers which mankind faces, and fire our hearts with a fresh vision of the necessity of Christ, his faith, his wisdom, and his goodness, if we are to be saved. Baptize thy Church with a Christlike care for the whole world, for its social ills, its public wrongs, its personal needs. And today, as we adore him in the sanctuary, may we one by one recall his words: "Not every one who says to me, 'Lord, Lord,' shall enter the kingdom of heaven, but he who does the will of my Father who is in heaven."

In the Spirit of Christ we pray. AMEN.

51

O GOD, from whom come all things good in man and nature, we would hospitably open our spirits to thee. Thou art everywhere present, yet in this sanctuary we would today more intimately find thee and be found by thee. Infinity of grace and goodness, lift us up into new faith in thee and a fresh vision of thee. The streams that overflow from thine abundance make life beautiful, yet dark hours come when unanswered questions rise and doubts throng in. We need reassurance, restored confidence, enlightened faith.

The beauty of nature, its symmetry and order, harmony and color—that we gratefully see. The virtues of human life at its best, integrity and honor, courage and good will—for that we are thankful. The achievements of man's mind and character, the truth that science seeks, the beauty that art creates, the goodness that high-minded men and women attain—by that we are enheartened. And for social victories, where light has risen out of darkness, love has proved stronger than hate, and what seemed impossible by thy grace has come true, we lift to thee our praise and gratitude.

O God, from whose vast reservoir of goodness these streams flow, make us more certain about thee, until today we too shall say, O God, thou art my God.

By this strengthened faith lift us up into refreshed courage. We pray for a Christian triumph over our social evils. Long ago on the mountaintop, O Christ, thou didst proclaim the sacred principles of thy holy faith; long ago thou didst die for man and rise in victory; and still thou seest man's cruelty to man. We confess our social sins that disgrace the earth. Yet, O Christ, thou dost haunt the conscience of the world. From all hopelessness and cynicism, from all skepticism and lack of faith, deliver us, and grant us courage to stand up for thee and serve well thy cause.

Thou seest with what varied needs thy children seek thee. O thou who dost meet us in the solitude of our souls, with thy still, small voice speak to us one by one. We have sinned, and we need the grace of sincere penitence and the cleansing mercy of thy pardon. If we are in grief, steady and comfort us; put beneath us thy strong foundations, that the storm of sorrow may not beat us down. If we are anxious and perplexed, shed light on our path. O God, unsnarl some tangled life in this worshiping company, we beseech thee, and send us out, our vision cleared, our faith confirmed, to be thy loyal servants.

Keep us from selfish living in this dangerous, difficult time, which cannot conquer its follies without public-mindedness. Raise up leaders in the church and nation, and call us all to play our part in attacking the evils which disgrace our country and the world. Especially we pray that thy hand of high commission may be laid on some young man or woman here. May some life find today its true vocation, and go out with loyal dedication to serve thee. So we would all open our hearts to thy transforming presence. Come, Spirit of the living God, and redeem us.

We pray in the name of Christ. AMEN.

52

ETERNAL GOD, the Shepherd of our souls, out of the noise of the world, its turbulence and its truculence, we come with reverence to worship thee. Refresh in us the spirit of wonder and awe. From things that man has made, we come into thy sanctuary to think of what thou hast made. Deepen in us reverence before this vast universe—the wonder of the stars, the glory of the sun, the march of the seasons, the procession of day and night. O God, from everlasting to everlasting, whose years never fail, mystery upon mystery is this life of ours, its background, its sustenance, and its destiny. In reverence and wonder we worship thee!

Give us a fresh vision, we beseech thee, of the Highest. Let Christ dawn upon us anew this day. Make everything that is excellent in life real to us. Break upon our dull sight with the vision of the ineffable and the beautiful that we may delight in life again and be thankful. Too easily we learn to despise life. We would learn to love it again this morning, to see that it is good, and to cry once more with all our hearts, "Serve the Lord with gladness."

We come before thee with deep regret for the wrongs that we have done. Many an opportunity we have wasted, and we have made a sad tale of what might have been a glorious story. We have left our friends sad when they should have been happy, depressed when they might have been elevated, dull when they ought to have been illumined. For all that has been wrong in us we repent, and acknowledge the reality of our human sin, that lies like a shadow across the face of the earth. Make more poignant within us the sense of our iniquities, personal and social. Send us out with firmer purpose and high resolve, with penitence and power.

We seek in thee depth and strength of character to handle

the joys and adversities of the days ahead. We ask thee for no more comfortable time; we know our destiny lies with hardship; but we pray for houses built upon sound foundations of enduring rock, that will not fall when the rains descend and the floods come and the winds blow. Let not prosperity spoil us or adversity shake us, but let joy be our opportunity and let trouble evoke the best in us, that we may be worthy, even though afar off, to be disciples of the Christ who took into his life alike the lilies of the field and the Cross on Calvary.

We lay before thee our deep solicitude about the world. O God, grant thy people intelligence, and the grace to use it for mankind's good! Not only our evil destroys humanity but our stupidity. We crucify Christ because we know not what we do. Save us from the insanity that throws away the gracious gifts of opportunity that are ours, devastating the earth with cruelty, when we might live in peace and plenty. May we learn to love the Lord our God with all our minds! Grant us wisdom in the leadership of the nations, and good will to follow it in the whole body of the people.

Come close to those in special need, and beyond the power of any petition to sum up our wants, be thou our adequate resource. Grant us zest in living that no grimness of the times can take away, and resilience of heart that no fear can destroy. So help us to bear living witness to the triumphant grace of Christ, in whose name we pray. AMEN.

53

ETERNAL SPIRIT, well of living water, harvest field from which comes the bread of life, we bring to thee our souls, thankful and needy, radiant and cast down, glad and penitent. Could we have lived by temporal bread alone we had not sought thee. Deep beneath the needs which earthly things can satisfy is the hunger which thou alone canst meet. Grant us such willing surrender and receptivity that to us may freely come the insight and wisdom, the grace and power, without which no man can fully live.

We pray for a courageous faith. Our fathers walked through days of tumult when the future was unsure. So walk we. Give us a creative faith such that thy Spirit in us, brooding over chaos, may bring order out of it. Grant us inward resources of spiritual power that we may be not submerged in difficulty but may rise above it, be superior to it, and carry off a spiritual triumph in the face of it. Make of us radiant, victorious personalities that shall commend to all the world the faith we profess.

We pray for vision. See how the blind lead the blind and fall into the ditch! Raise up for this people, we beseech thee, leaders who shall see a little way ahead and know what our people ought to do. In our personal estate grant us insight that shall make plainer the path before us until problems grow less complex and duties more clear. We have come to thee, thou source of light, that we might be children of the light and not walk in darkness. Therefore grant vision to thy servants' inner eyes. We pray for eternal horizons around our daily duties. We grow obsessed with difficulties and tasks near at hand until our perspectives become narrow and our horizons shut us in. Lift us up to a far outlook. Upon the bleak hills that surround some souls today put horses and chariots of fire. Expand our sympathies, overflow our doubts, increase our faith! Lift us to such an altitude that we may go forth from this place new men and new women in a new world.

We ask thee for no soft comfort. We request of thee not life made easy but inward fortification. Especially we pray for those in perplexity over their practical estate. We cannot live by bread alone but we cannot live without it. When, not for ourselves only but for our families and friends, the human need is clamorous, canst thou measure our agony? Open the free channels of good will among this people. Touch our generosity until like a fountain it shall overflow. Grant that even as we pray for those hurt by penury we may have imagination to see them and unselfishness to assist them.

We beseech thee also for those hard pressed by moral temptation. O God, the upward path is very steep for human feet. It is easier to go down than to rise. Surround some spirit in thy presence here with thy protective care. Remind us in time that it is easier to prevent evil than to recover from it. Save us from dishonoring our lives. So challenge us with the need of the world that we may contribute to it at least one good life, adventurous for righteousness.

So in personal want, in family perplexity, in secret temptation, in earnest desire for thy Kingdom on earth, we commit ourselves to thee, in the Spirit of Christ. AMEN.

54

Eternal Spirit from whom we come, to whom we belong, and in whose fellowship is our peace, we worship thee. Thou art never far from us but often we are very far from thee. From the tumult of the world and the preoccupation of its many tasks, from its noise and strife, our spirits turn again for peace, insight, power, to the quiet of thy sanctuary. Make thou our hearts a shrine. Build there thine altar. Kindle there thy fire.

Grant unto us more sensitive consciences. If we have sinned against those who trust us, if smoke from our lives has clouded another sky, if by careless temper and unhappy word we have made it harder for others either to do good or to know joy, do thou forgive us. Make us sensitive and keep us from hardness and callousness.

Refresh in us the first loves that made our families. Kindle anew in us the beauty of the parental relationship. Let friendship grow real to us again. May the fellowship of thy Church surround us with a great cloud of witnesses, confirming our faith and ennobling our characters. If amid the noises of the world the calm voice of whatever is excellent and true and good has been difficult to hear, now in the quiet of thy sanctuary speak thou to us and may we say to thee, "thy servant heareth."

Grant us appreciative souls. If the hardships of the world have embittered us until its benedictions have been half forgotten, remind us, we pray thee, of all the spiritual assets of life. Make real to us again the background out of which we have come, the nobler aspects of our heritage, the resources of power within our reach, the friends that have not been untrue, the families that have not been unkind. Refresh our hope and courage.

As thus we pray for ourselves, we present in our vicarious intercession all spirits everywhere who pray to thee. Though they use not our roads to thee, though their words are not our words nor their names for thee our names, yet come thou into every open and prayerful heart that seeks thy grace. Grant a revival of spiritual life to our needy world, transforming our souls and societies, and saving us from the perils of our waywardness and sin.

We pray for those who cannot pray for themselves, the embittered, who have seen so little goodness in human life that they cannot believe in thy goodness, until they are alienated from their own peace and righteousness. For them we pray. We take their burden on our consciences. We acknowledge our social responsibility for them. We have had a hand in building this human world whose iniquities and cruelties so have hurt the souls of our fellows. We dare not stand aloof as though they were sinners and we righteous. We repent before thee because of them.

Especially we beseech thee for the peace of the world. Save us not only from our sins but from our follies. Teach us the futility and insanity of violence. Lead us under wise and strong guidance into ways of peace and decency, humaneness and brotherhood. To that end cleanse thou our own hearts. Let all malice and anger and wrath and evil speaking be put away from us, and beyond our power to ask let the peace of God that passeth all understanding stand guard over our hearts this day.

We pray in the Spirit of Christ.   AMEN.

55

ETERNAL GOD, who art before all, in all, and beyond all, we worship thee. Enlarge our thoughts of thee. Deepen our insight into thy character, revealed in Christ. We stand in awe before this universe in which thou hast housed us. We bow in reverence before its Creator, the heights and depths of whose power and purpose we cannot comprehend. Such knowledge is too wonderful for us; it is high, we cannot attain unto it.

Thanks be to thee for the revelation of thyself in prophets and apostles, saints and martyrs, in all that is excellent and beautiful, and above all in Jesus Christ, our Lord. May some light from thee fall upon our souls today. Search us, O God, and know our hearts! Try us and know our thoughts! And see if there be any wicked way in us, and lead us in the way everlasting.

We pray for thy help in all the innermost relationships of our lives. Guide us in our dealing with ourselves. O thou who hearest the endless conversation wherein we talk with ourselves, give us sincerity, honesty, and candor as we deal with ourselves. Save us from the folly of self-deceit. Grant us grace to see ourselves as we really are, to hate those evil things in us which we ought to hate, and to appraise rightly those powers in us wherewith we can best serve man and thee.

We pray for thy help in our relationships with our fellows. Against all vindictiveness, all malice of heart and unkindness in conduct, we pray. Save us from meanness of spirit and from the love of retaliation. Make us a source of strength and encouragement to those whom we love, and grant us grace to overthrow our enemies by transforming them into our friends. May some human relationships be made radiant and be filled with good will because we have worshiped here today.

We pray for thy help in our relationships with thee. Make our Christian faith and life vital because it is centered in inner fellowship and communion with thy Spirit. May we indeed be thy temples with thy Spirit dwelling in us. From the uproar of the world to the silent sanctuary we have come. Speak to us, O still, small voice of calm. Become to us our unseen Friend, our Comrade in life's battles, our Shelter in the time of storm, our Wellspring of courage and steadfastness.

We lift our intercession for this needy world and especially for its peace and brotherhood. Father in heaven, thy frail children here on earth find it hard to believe in good will when ill will is so powerful. When racial prejudice not only works hatred in private hearts but is erected into the policy of states, when powerful nations prey upon weaker nations because they can, when class is arrayed against class in fratricidal strife, lo! the Christ still stands teaching us good will. Lord, we believe; help thou our unbelief! Let some word be spoken in thy sanctuary that shall restore our souls to a living confidence in the eternal power of love at last to subdue the angry voices of mankind's ill will and build a family on earth.

Now take our church and this worshiping company into thy keeping. For all the children who have come to our doors today we thank thee. Make us worthy to be entrusted with their growing lives. For those upon whom sickness has come, and homes on which bereavement has laid its shadow, we pray to thee. For all hard bestead by ill circumstances we pray thee, and grant that where our hearts go in supplication our hands may go in practical helpfulness. Send us out into the world with souls restored because we have been strengthened and enlightened by thy grace.

Through Jesus Christ we make our prayer. AMEN.

56

ETERNAL GOD, who knowest our necessities before we ask, and our ignorance in asking, we come in the fellowship of prayer to seek light upon our ways and strength within our hearts. In awe and reverence we bow before thy greatness which we cannot measure. Like creatures of the sea that feel the impulse of the tides, not understanding them, so are we amid the majestic movements of thy Providence. Like birds upon the wing, should they question the air in which they fly, so are we when we question thee. Alpha and Omega, the Beginning and the Ending, wherever we flee from thy Spirit, thou art around us and far beyond us.

Thanks be to thee that thou also art within us. Our eyes have seen beauty, our hearts have felt love, our minds have discovered truth, our wills have found purposes that ennoble life, and deep in our souls thou hast been to us like a spring of water welling up to eternal life. O Spirit within, as well as without, grant us now an hour of fellowship with thee, that shall bring to our souls radiance and insight, peace and power.

We turn to thee from the perplexities of daily life, and pray for relief from disquieting and cowardly fears. Bewildered by the world's confusion, we lose certitude and stability. We are tempted by petty annoyances and great griefs, by despondency and doubt, and by the angry emotions of our time. Restore to thy servants the sanity and courage we sorely need, and banish our evil by the expulsive power of new faith, new affections, and new desires.

We pray especially for guidance in a Christlike way of life. The devices of the world entice us; the sophistries of the cynical and the inclinations of our own hearts tempt us; and evil solicitations silence our consciences with their subtle persuasion. Grant us true penitence and sincere amendment of life. Help us to see the right and to love it. Fortify our decision to live with honesty, integrity, and unselfishness.

We pray for all Christian churches around the world. From the tyranny of old customs and ideas, once helpful but now outgrown, good Lord deliver us. From stressing the trivial and forgetting the vital, save thy people. Grant thy Church a new reformation, and may she both proclaim the Gospel and live it so that the minds of men may be convinced, their lives be transformed, their societies be redeemed. Open the gates of a new morning before thy Church, and grant her fresh hopes of unity, fresh depths of vital faith, and fresh devotion to thy Kingdom's coming.

Guide our nation in these difficult days. Use our power for thy purposes of justice and peace. Save us from selfish nationalism. Save us from our racial prejudice and discrimination, which destroy our influence for good around the world. May our help bring hope to depressed and stricken lands, where despotism reigns, where the liberty of human souls is stolen from them, where poverty afflicts the people, where the spirit and teaching of Christ are trodden underfoot. Strengthen the United Nations and all agencies dedicated to mankind's peace, and grant that our eyes may see the victory of our Lord, Christ Jesus, over the enemies of his truth.

O God, our words when we pray are but small cups dipped from the deep lake of our need. Look thou upon our want, deeper than our words, and give to each of us according to his need and to the riches of thy grace in Christ. AMEN.

PRAYERS
FOR
SPECIAL
OCCASIONS

New Year's Sunday [1]

ETERNAL GOD, before the mountains were brought forth or ever thou hadst formed the earth and the world, even from everlasting to everlasting thou art God. A thousand years in thy sight are but as yesterday when it is past and as a watch in the night. We, thy transient children on this earth, would set our lives against the background of thine everlastingness, there to learn humility, there to find inner stability and peace.

Grant us insight and vision that we may behold things seen as temporal and things unseen as eternal. Our lives are shallow; we need depth. Our lives are fretful and irritated; we need quietude and serenity. O God, throw thy greatness about us, and round our restlessness thy rest.

We come to thee at the year's passing with thankful hearts. For all that crowns life with beauty and blessedness we are grateful. Quicken our thanksgiving for the benedictions of family and friends, for books and music that inspire us, for our costly heritage in church and nation, for all the present blessings that gladden our hearts. If we came here careless or cynical, send us out rejoicing and grateful.

We come to thee with penitence for the sorry failures that spoil our recollections of the year gone by. We have been thoughtless and unkind when good will would have helped a friend. We have filled other lives with our smoke, darkening days that else might have been sun-clear. Surrendering to our worst, we have made it difficult for others to live at their best. We are sinners, Lord, and we confess it. O God, grant us such sincere penitence and such effectual desire for amendment, that through the gateway of another year we may pass forgiven and empowered.

We bring to thee our care for the new year and its manifold interests. We would build for our children a more decent, humane, and brotherly world. Grant us fresh faith and courage for the task. Often our hearts are cast down within us. Life is full of mystery. We look out across it as across a stormy ocean where clouds lie thick and billows rise high. If we have grown discouraged, undergird us with fresh confidence for life's high enterprise, and send us out into this new year with restored determination and devotion.

If the Eternal were against us, then were all our works vain and our hopes empty. Thanks be to thee, O God, for the great tradition of our faith, the insights of the seers, the visitations of the Divine in our own hearts, and Christ above all, thy very word spoken to us in a life, assuring us that the eternal is not only great but good, and that where love is there God is also. Strengthen us with this faith renewed to-day for the year that awaits us. Undergird all the uncertainty of its perplexing days and its disturbed circumstance with a steady confidence in thine eternal Purpose. O God of goodness and of grace, be our God now!

Gather us all into thy sustaining care. The children with their eagerness and gaiety—let thy benediction rest on them. The youths with their growing strength—enrich their lives with worthy interests. The mature in the fullness of their power—may they use it with dedicated unselfishness. The aged who draw near the end of their journey—may the gates of death be to them open doors to an eternal morning. All of us, facing our temptations, trials, challenges, and opportunities—make us adequate for each day's living. So, beyond our power to ask or our right to deserve, minister thou in secret to our souls.

We pray in the Spirit of Christ. AMEN.

New Year's Sunday   [2]

ETERNAL SPIRIT, whom no man by searching can find out, seek us and find us out, we pray. We would worship thee with hospitable hearts, welcoming thee to our minds and lives. Come, knock on the door and give us grace to open. Come to us in stimulating thoughts, clear insights, and illumined faith, in moving gratitude that makes us humble, in penitence that cleanses us, in a sense of vocation that challenges us. Come to us in a fresh vision of Christ, his grace and mercy, his call to our consciences, and his appeal to our strength.

As thus amid the earthquake, wind, and fire of this noisy world we wait for thy still, small voice, give us sensitive hearts to listen, teachable minds to learn, humble wills to obey. Here today let some revelation of thy light fall on our darkness, some guidance from thy wisdom save us in our bewilderment, some power from thine infinite resource strengthen us in our need.

For special help we pray as an old year ends and the unknown future, full of danger, yet full of possibilities, opens before us. Make us great enough for these great days! Against all our sins that defeat thy holy purpose we pray, but especially against the sins of littleness, meanness, prejudice, provincialism. Cast down our pride, national, racial, personal. Make us humble, understanding, co-operative members of our one humanity. Lift us above the petty to grasp the import of these momentous times, and thus to help build that one world, missing which our children will face chaos and catastrophe.

For all who labor in church and state this coming year to bring sense and system into our disordered world, we pray with anxious hearts. Let no failures so frighten them, no difficulties so dishearten them or us, who stand behind them, that they surrender to defeat. And when another new year comes, God grant that our eyes may look upon a better world traveling a highway toward peace and brotherhood.

With gratitude we remember in our intercession those loyal servants to whose ministries we are unpayably indebted: physicians and nurses, the teachers in our schools, devoted men and women in law and business, homemakers and social workers, missionaries in far places, and friendly souls close at hand whose good will and radiance illumine and sustain us.

For ourselves one by one we pray that we may be among the world's assets and not its liabilities. For strength to stand up in trouble, for courage to overcome temptation, for inward grace from divine resources to master life and not be mastered by it, we pray to thee. Through joy and sorrow, success and failure, the world's favor and the world's enmity, through happy fellowship with those we love and through bereavement when the bell tolls for them and us, God keep us steadfast, undefeated, undishonored, unashamed.

Let the light shine on all of us today, making plain some answers to our questions, some assurance for our doubts, some strength for our weakness, some vision of our duty, and may we be the more valiant and triumphant spirits because we have worshiped thee here, in the Spirit of Christ.   AMEN.

Epiphany

ETERNAL SPIRIT, who art ever more ready to hear than we are to pray, who knowest our necessities before we ask, and our ignorance in asking, behold us here, seeking in a common prayer light upon our ways, and strength within our hearts. Give us the listening ear, the responsive will, and bring such answer to each sincere prayer, as each of us severally needs.

We turn to thee from the perplexities and uncertainties which daily beset us, and pray for relief from disquieting and cowardly fears. We are bewildered by the confusion of the world. We lose the way of certitude and self-control. We are tempted by petty annoyances, by despondency and doubt, and by the angry emotions of the world. The fear of doing wrong paralyzes the power to do right, and our decisions falter under the strain of apprehension and self-distrust. Restore to thy servants the sanity and courage they sorely need, and banish the evil spirit of fear by the expulsive power of new faith, new affections, and new desires.

O Lord, beset as we are by misleading counsels and wicked practices, we pray for guidance in a straight way of life. The devices and duplicity of the world are familiar and enticing, the sophistries of the cynical, and the inclinations of our own hearts to self-deceit tempt us to lose the road, and many evil solicitations silence our consciences by their subtle persuasion. Give us, we pray, a firmer hold on thine immutable laws of righteousness. Search our hearts and drive from them all indirection, equivocation, and pretense. Fortify our decision to live with sincerity, tranquillity, and self-effacement. Like the wise men at the first Epiphany, may we find Christ and adore him.

As thus we seek reinforcement and rectitude for our own lives, it is for the world's sake we pray. We would be true servants of thy will in this troubled time. For this war-torn earth, devastated by violence, we lift our penitent and anxious supplication. Tyranny and hatred rule the world; the light of learning is put out; the liberty of human souls is taken from them; the hopes of the young are destroyed; and the Spirit and teaching of Christ, in whom alone is hope for men and nations, are trampled underfoot.

Guide our nation in these days of difficult decision. Lord God Omnipotent, who art above all nations, use us for thy purposes; work in us a moving penitence and amendment of life; save us from the anarchy of unbridled nationalism; teach us alike the necessity and the wisdom of learning to be all one family, and through these turbulent days keep our minds and spirits steady. Especially may thy Church be true to her high vocation, that out of the world's travail there may come a new birth of hope and justice and good will among men.

Now come close to hearts so troubled over their private griefs that they can hardly feel the grief of the world. See how, discouraged and bereaved, smitten down and weary with life some of thy servants are! We pray for a new spirit of triumph and hope. Thou canst send us out today saying, "Bless the Lord, O my soul!" Thou canst reveal to us resources of power adequate to make us more than conquerors! For that we pray in the Spirit of Christ! AMEN.

First Sunday in Lent

ETERNAL SPIRIT, who at the first didst brood over chaos and bring order from it, brood, we beseech thee, over our souls. For our lives are disordered and amid the pressures of this present world lose their meaning, direction, and aim. We need deep faith to undergird us, high hopes to allure us, profound resources to strengthen us. Brood, we beseech thee, over thy waiting and worshiping people; draw our lives together and make them whole.

Give us grace to look deeply inward. From the immediate and external turn our eyes within. For the world is too much with us and we forget that while we have bodies we are souls. So minister to our inner life that we may have strength to rise above its temptations, to stand strong in the midst of its dismaying troubles, and to keep faith, courage, and honor high even when the world seems against us, that we may prosper even as our souls prosper.

Give us the grace to look not only inward but upward. O God, let not the uplook of our spirits fail us in a day when the outlook is so dismaying. Let not God be lost to us. May we feel ourselves in thine inescapable hands and to our clear vision may the hills appear from whence our help cometh. On this first Sunday of the Lenten season we remember our Lord in the days of his temptation, withstanding the evil one and saying, "You shall worship the Lord your God and him only shall you serve." So may our eyes steadfastly look up to thee, and our lives be disciplined and directed by our devotion to the Highest.

Give us grace to look not only inward and upward but outward. Let our brothers come into the scope and horizon of our prayers. Let us bear our own troubles that we may be better able to help them in theirs. If we are in desolation, steady us for their sakes, and if we are in prosperity, shame us from our selfish ease that we may remember them in their frailty and need. Because we have worshiped here let some fair consequence come to other souls through the overflow of our generosity and affection.

God help us also to look forward. Let not hope fail thy servants in these days. For all the realism with which we see the actual, let not thy servants forget the possible in ourselves, in our fellows, in our society. Let not the dream which has sustained the prophets, that the Kingdom of thy grace and righteousness shall come on earth, fade because of lost faith or discouragement of heart. Make us strong in a day when we are tempted to be weak and hopeful in a day when we are tempted to be disheartened, that we may be part of that saving minority of thine approved people from whom at last shall come peace and brotherhood and justice among men.

Now come close to us one by one, for how can we make a good world out of evil folk? We would cleanse our own lives and have them by thy grace redeemed and reinforced. Thou art always near us, yet by our insensitiveness we shut thee out. During this Lenten season quicken our awareness of thy presence, and to thy Spirit within us make us receptive and hospitable. O world invisible, in which we really live, be real to us today, and in that inner fellowship may there come peace out of anxiety, steadfastness out of turmoil, forgiveness out of guilt, strength out of weakness, faith instead of fear.

We ask it in the Spirit of Christ. AMEN.

Palm Sunday

ETERNAL SPIRIT, thou unseen source of peace and power, we worship thee. Oft we have strayed from thy straight path, walking not kindly with one another, or humbly with thee, or honorably with ourselves, afraid of that which we should not fear, and seeking that which we should not desire. We come to thee for thy correction and redemption. Arise within our hearts, thou fountain of all grace, with cleansing pardon, healing strength, steadying resource, and overflowing joy.

Father of light, we bless thee for the brave men and women who have gone before us, by whose example we have been enheartened and from whose sacrificial living we have profited. We bless thee for the duties of life, its loyalties and obligations, its responsibilities and tasks, from which if thou wilt sustain us in faithful stewardship, satisfying meaning and purpose shall flow into our living. We bless thee for the love of our friends, the beauty of our homes, the entrustment of children, and for every window of affection and good will through which light falls upon our lives.

Especially, we remember, with the gratitude of those who have been redeemed, the life of him who for our sakes died on Calvary. We confess our infidelity to him, we who like ancient Jerusalem have often welcomed him with protestations of loyalty, and ere the week ended have crucified him. Amid the waywardness of a violent world, that has denied his faith and forsaken his way, we turn afresh to him. To whom else can we go; he has the words of eternal life. Grant us a fresh vision of his way of living, a resolute decision to let him be our Master, and a new willingness daily to take up our cross and follow him.

In the light of his life and teaching, his death and victory, quicken our consciences that we may feel the sin and shame of man's inhumanity to man. Inspire us with insight and courage that we may combat private greed, social injustice, intolerance and bigotry, the ills of poverty, the misuses of power, and whatever else works enmity between man and man, class and class, race and race, nation and nation. We are sickened by the cries of hatred and the crimes of violence. We see no hope in war piled on war, and bloodshed forever answered by more bloodshed still. O Christ, our Lord, who didst bring to thy first disciples, frightened and dismayed by thy crucifixion, such victorious assurance of thy living presence and power, we need thee now. Say to us once more, "In the world you have tribulation; but be of good cheer, I have overcome the world."

For all ministers of hope and good will in the world's dark places, for all who feed the hungry, relieve the poor, and heal the sick, we pray. For every candle lighted in a benighted land, for every exemplar of good will amid ill will, and of humane service amid cruel need, we thank thee. May the dark places of the earth be illumined by our gifts also, and may thy Church, unshaken in faith and unspoiled in spirit by man's ungodliness, still lift her testimony for the Christ, who died that the world might be saved.

In his name we pray. AMEN.

Easter Sunday [1]

ETERNAL GOD, before whom the morning stars first sang together, and who holdest in thy hands the destiny of every living thing, we worship thee. Thanks be to thee for the note of victory that fills our souls today! Thanks to thee for our living Lord over whom death had no dominion! For the rich heritage of faith that life is ever lord of death, and that love can never lose its own, we thank thee. Strengthen our believing. Confirm our confidence in thee and life eternal.

We thank thee for all things excellent and beautiful that make faith in immortality more sure. For our friends who have loved us, our homes that have nourished us, for the heights and depths of the human spirit, full of promise and prophecy, for all victories of right over wrong, and above all for Christ, who has brought life and immortality to light, we thank thee. Join to our company today those whom we have loved and who live with thee in the house not made with hands. Gather us into the fellowship of the Church, both militant and triumphant, as we sing praise to thee.

We pray for those defeated souls to whom the note of victory sounds distant and unreal. Thou seest them here, known to thee though not to us, spirits frustrated by circumstance, overwhelmed by temptation, facing griefs too heavy for their unaided strength. O thou, who canst make the barren place rejoice and the desert to blossom like the rose, redeem some stricken souls here from defeat to victory.

Replenish with new hope all who are discouraged about the world, who find faith in the ultimate victory of righteousness difficult. So often might triumphs over right, and the good is undone by evil that, like our Master on his Cross we cry, "My God, my God, why hast thou forsaken me?" O thou to whom a thousand years are but as yesterday when it is past, and as a watch in the night, speak to us and refresh our souls with a new hope. Lift our vision above the immediate; illumine for us that eternal purpose which thou didst purpose in Christ. Say to us this Easter day that no Calvary can finally defeat Christ.

We lay before thee our concern for thy Church. For the great tradition of her strong and saving faith, thanks be to thee. Draw her members together into increasing unity. Grant that in these days of danger and opportunity her Gospel of deathless hope, of unconquerable faith, of invincible courage, may inspire thy people. Send us out from this high hour of worship to be fearless and faithful citizens of thy Kingdom.

To that end may the living Christ be not only in our creed but in our experience. Let not Easter day represent to us only an historic victory; may it mean a present triumph in our souls—the living Christ our inspiration and our strength, so that we live, and yet not we, but Christ lives in us, the hope of glory. In that sustaining faith may we, too, like our Master, overcome the world.

We pray in the name of Christ.   AMEN.

Easter Sunday   [2]

O GOD, Lord of all worlds, seen and unseen, transient and eternal, we worship thee. Soul of the universe, Creator of our bodies, Father of our spirits, to thee we turn for strength and peace. We are children of a day; our sun has its rising and its setting; yet deep within our hearts is the instinct of immortality, and the reach of our souls is beyond the grasp of our hands.

O thou, who has so mysteriously made us that, living in the midst of the temporal, we still think thoughts that lay hold upon eternity, we trust in thee. Thy promises are written in our hearts. We will believe them. What eye hath not seen, nor ear heard, and what hath not entered into the heart of man, thou hast laid up for them that love thee. Give us eyes today to see the open road ahead, and touch our spirits with the radiant hope of life eternal.

Thanks be to thee for Christ our Lord, for the beauty and strength of his life, the truth of his teaching, his powerful influence upon the world, the nobility of his sacrificial death, and for his victory! Thanks be to thee for his life, continued in the house not made with hands, and in those who welcome his spirit in their souls! On Calvary death slew life, and yet life was conqueror; hatred slew love and love triumphed; evil slew goodness and goodness proved the stronger. Fill our hearts today with the joy of his victory.

Thanks be to thee for those souls whom we have loved long since and lost awhile. Their lives were dear to us; their names are precious in our memories. Fathers and mothers, husbands and wives, children and friends, we remember them today. Spirit of the living God, walk among this people and see the priceless loves and loyalties cherished in our hearts, the invisible presences who worship with us. Let us not be a company of those alone clad in the body, but bring the company of unseen witnesses about us. Ah, Lord, no harm must come to them. The souls of the righteous are in thy hands. Keep them whom we have committed unto thee against that day.

We bring to thee the world that needs thee. Would that we could sing a song about love's victory there, but still we are, as our fathers were before us on the earth, the Church militant, not yet the Church triumphant. Lord, make us to be the Church militant in nobility of spirit and sacrifice of life. Touch us with the needs of the needy, with the suffering of the aggrieved, with the hurt of those who are under tyranny. Touch us with loyalty to great causes that death cannot stop and wrong cannot conquer. Make us the Church militant for peace against war, for righteousness against injustice, for love against hate, for generosity against ill will.

Come close to each one of us, and beyond the power of any human prayer, meet thou our secret inner needs. Especially come to those upon whose lips the song of triumph languishes today, who see no sunshine breaking through the clouds on their shadowed lives. Make some spirit radiant today that had not expected it; surprise with hope some who have not dared to harbor it; bring life to some whose spirits are already dead, and from the grave of self-defeat let there be a resurrection here of love, and joy, and strength.

We ask it in the Spirit of the Christ. AMEN.

Whitsunday (Pentecost)

Holy Spirit of God, who at Pentecost didst descend with power upon Christ's disciples and didst send them out to preach the Gospel and to found the Church, inspire us also to sustain what they began. O Most High, mean to us what thou didst mean to them: the grace of our Lord Jesus Christ, the love of God, and the fellowship of the Holy Spirit. Enrich our souls with that threefold experience, that thou mayest be to us the Almighty Creator, the Saving Character, the Indwelling Comforter.

Eternal Spirit, mysterious beyond our understanding, yet shining clearly in all that is excellent and true, we deeply need thy help. We are not sufficient unto ourselves. As we did not create ourselves, so we cannot sustain ourselves amid life's strains and anxieties, storms and temptations, disappointments and griefs. Here we would lay aside all pride, and humbly acknowledge our urgent need. For light enough to walk by through dark days, for inner strength to carry heavy burdens, undertake courageous deeds, sustain personal sorrow, and render faithful service to our generation, we pray to thee. Spirit of the Eternal, make us more than ourselves, because we have thee for our ally and reinforcement.

Baptize us with the grace of appreciation. Enlarge our capacities for joy. Forgive us that we miss so many opportunities to be glad and grateful. Open our hearts to happiness in simple things, to mirth that has no bitter springs and no sad aftermath. In the beauty of nature, in human friendship, in family life, in the joys of common tasks and familiar relationships, may we find satisfaction, that we may live not only with integrity but with radiance.

We thank thee for the heritage which is ours in Christ, and for the great tradition that thy Church has handed down to us. Make us worthy of our inheritance. Let us not because of any infidelity or lack of character hurt it by our mishandling, or rob our children of its full possession. We pray for another Pentecost, another outpouring of thy Spirit on thy Church. For still the peoples of the earth wander like sheep without a shepherd. Still earthly riches leave them destitute in soul, and by the very things their ingenious minds invent their spirits are wounded and the hopes of mankind are threatened. Still tyranny oppresses multitudes, the liberty of human souls is taken from them, the hopes of the young are destroyed, and the Spirit and teaching of Christ are trampled underfoot. O God, awaken thy Church. Raise up leaders, prophets in thy pulpits, teachers in the schools, statesmen in seats of government, and enlighten and inspire thy Church throughout the world.

We pray thee for venturesome and courageous spirits. Save us from our timidities and fears, from the reluctance and paralysis of our uncertainties and doubts. Nerve us, we beseech thee, that with noble tasks to be enterprised and done, we may be strong to endure, to sacrifice, and to achieve. Since thou hast done us this high honor, calling us into an unfinished world to bear a hand with thee in its completion, give us wisdom and strength that we may work while it is day, ere the night comes, when no man can work.

We pray in the name of Christ. AMEN.

Thanksgiving Day   [1]

ETERNAL SPIRIT, high above yet deep within us all, we gather on this day, dedicated to gratitude, to worship thee. Thanks be to thee for all interior resources of power by which the spirit, even in the midst of this tumultuous world, can nobly live. Thanks to thee for the inward shepherding which can lead us in green pastures and beside still waters, restoring the soul.

For the privilege of the shut door, the quiet hour of tranquillity, and the peace gained in high companionship with thee, for all that the spirit can do with its own solitariness, thanks be to thee. In thy sanctuary today, even more deeply, we thank thee for fellowship. With gratitude we lift in thy presence the remembrance of our friends. In our imaginations again we see their faces, in our minds we think their names. For their comfort in the day of trouble, stability in a time of confusion, guidance when we were bewildered, inspiration when we were downcast, gracing our lives with beauty and crowning them with joy, thanks be to thee.

Thanks be to thee for that wider circle of friends from all generations whom we have not seen in the flesh but have met in the spirit. For the interior fellowship of great souls through whom thou hast blessed the world—prophets, apostles, martyrs, creators of beauty, discoverers of truth—who as soon as we are born begin to be our friends and with whom we can walk in an ennobling fellowship, thanks be to thee.

Thanks be to thee for the fellowship of our homes. Thou seest how deeply our care for them lies in our hearts and how dear are the faces that our imaginations picture and our spirits love. O God, be merciful as we pray for our families, for the love that sustains them, for the children that go forth from them, and for all the ties of affection and memory and hope that make them beautiful.

Thanks be to thee for the fellowship of the Church. Imperfect people, we build imperfect churches, yet our gratitude ascends to thee for the ministry of thy Church, which has brought to us so rich a heritage and inspirations that have elevated our common lives to altitudes else impossible. For the great tradition of thy Gospel and the corporate testimony of thy saints we thank thee.

We beseech thee for fellowships sadly broken in the earth. Forgive us for sundered nations and divided races and embittered classes. Thou great Friend of man, whose dearest wish is the friednship of thy people, beget in us so true a spirit of good will that we may build at last, though it be through sacrifice, a friendly world.

We lift in our petition those who can be helped by no earthly friendship only. So curiously hast thou made us that the soul, though set among many human helpers, is still a lonely traveler on this planet. Temptations are here that must be faced alone and troubles that must be borne alone. For all problems that thy people face in the solitude of their souls we pray to thee. Thou great friend of all the sons of men, let not thy friendship fail us. When most we seem to be alone, people the solitude with the presence of the Unseen Companion, the invisible Friend of our pilgrimage, and make us strong in the Spirit of Christ. Grant us a Thanksgiving Day when all that is within us shall praise the Lord. AMEN.

Thanksgiving Day   [2]

ETERNAL GOD, who art the God of all the universe beside, be also our God. For often we worship other gods that we have made with our own hands. Today help us to turn from our idolatries and worship thee. We would wait upon thee and be of good courage, for thou shalt strengthen our hearts.

Be thou the God of our private lives. Walk through the secret corridors of our souls. Blow through us, thou wind of God; shine through us, thou sun of righteousness. Make us wholesome and clean. Forgive our sins. Strengthen us in our temptations. Establish us in the midst of our anxieties. Be thou to us in the deep and secret places of our hearts our God indeed.

Be thou the God of our families. O thou who settest the solitary in households, we bless thee for our homes. Amid the news of broken households, amid the scandals that fly from lip to lip and flood like a torrent through the public press, we thank thee for the unheralded families that are wholesome and beautiful. For fathers and mothers who have reared us in the nurture and admonition of the Lord, for wives and husbands who have found through the years the stream of their love growing deeper and fuller, for children who are our pride and joy, blessed be God from whom every family in heaven and on earth is named!

Be thou the God of our nation! We thank thee for the heritage that thou hast given us in this country, so throned in richness between the seas. For the richness of our country-sides and the wealth of our resources we thank thee. Give us the grace, we beseech thee, in this land, to transcend our prosperity, to be superior to our wealth, to make it minister and not master, the servant of the spiritual life of this people. And in this day, alike of opportunity and crisis, when forces reach up from below and reach down from above to the corruption of our public life, we pray thee against the apathy and carelessness of our people. As thou hast given us a great heritage, help us to be true to it.

O God, be thou the God of our churches. We bless thee for them and for every just and excellent thing, august and of good report, that has come into our lives from them. We pray thee against their futility, against their triviality, against the ideas that cramp them and the divisions that enfeeble them. Raise up prophets in our time. Kindle their message with coals from off thine altar. Save us from misrepresenting the Son of God and the Lord of Glory, and make us more truly in our churches to be witnesses for him.

O God of mercy, as we celebrate our national thanksgiving, we beseech thee that we may be deeply grateful for all the benedictions that make life beautiful. But especially we pray thee for those who at Thanksgiving time will find it hard to be thankful. For those hard bestead with difficulty, oppressed by anxiety, brokenhearted with bereavement, disillusioned with disappointment, whose words of gratitude will be stayed upon their lips as Thanksgiving comes—we pray thee for them. If some today are sorely tried in their temptations, or can hardly look up to thee and pray because the heavens are brazen above them, grant on this day when thou hast flooded the outer world with thy sunshine some beam of grace and hope upon their discouragement. So minister to us in our worship beyond the power of our lips to ask. Be thou our God according to our need, and send us forth from this place no longer downcast, but saying, "Bless the Lord, O my soul: and all that is within me, bless his holy name."

We ask it for Christ's sake. AMEN.

First Sunday in Advent

ETERNAL SPIRIT, into the calm of thy presence we bring our restless lives. Silence the too great noise of our living. Quiet the turmoil of our stormy spirits. Smooth the irritations of our vexed hearts. Let quietness and responsiveness open our doors to thee. We need to be hushed that we may hear the Highest speak.

Speak to our consciences, we pray thee. May an arresting word from thee stop some soul here who is traveling a wrong road. Show us the falsity of our excuses and evasions, and grant us an hour of honest dealing with ourselves and thee. From our ill tempers, our unkind moods, our hasty words, our cherished vindictiveness, good Lord, deliver us. In the quiet of this hour may we be born again into a better mind and a more worthy life.

Speak to us in memory, we pray thee. May recollections of the homes from which we have come, of friends whose affection and fidelity have sustained us, of sacred hours when we have been certain of thy guiding hand, cleanse and reassure our hearts. Above all in this Advent season may the light of the knowledge of thy glory, which we have seen in the face of Jesus Christ, our Lord, stir us all to gratitude and devotion. Thanks be to thee for him, for his coming to redeem us, for his life and teaching, for his tragedy and his triumph. He is the way and the truth and the life—O God, make that not only our belief, but our conviction and our experience.

Speak to us in our hopes and our ideals, we pray thee. Save us from conformity with the low standards of the world. Grant us higher thoughts of Christ's purpose for us, a nobler philosophy of life's meaning, loftier goals for our devotion, worthier aims for our aspiration. Because we have worshiped thee here, may the character and mission of Jesus, the ends for which he lived and died, grow vivid in our thought. Beget hope in us that, by thy grace, we may rise above our meaner selves, outgrow our littleness, and render some Christlike service to the world.

Speak to our wills, we pray thee. O God, who hast given us the power of decision, whereby we can take either the right way or the wrong, can choose either the blessing or the curse, may we choose life and not death. To some soul here today, standing at the parting of the ways, may thy guidance come. May some decisions be made here whose fair fruition will make future years useful and joyful. Especially if thou art calling some youth to Christian life and service, grant him courage to say, "Here am I; send me."

Speak to us through the need of the world, we pray thee. We believe in thee, but how can we believe in man? The corruption of his life, the viciousness and violence of his deeds, tempt us to disgust and cynicism. Create in us fresh faith in mankind. Help us to look on men and women with the merciful eyes of Christ. Thou Son of God, whom men crucified, and yet who didst believe in man, in his possibility and destiny, send us out from our worship restored in confidence that justice can conquer greed, that peace can overcome war, that love is stronger than hate, that life is mightier than death.

We pray in thy name.   AMEN.

Christmas Sunday [1]

ETERNAL SPIRIT, to whom all souls belong, we lift our adoration and our praise to thee. Thanks be to thee for every gift of grace that elevates and enlightens life. Thou who didst surprise the world at Bethlehem, coming in a little babe, when none was so expecting thee, surprise us with some unforeseen arrival of thy help today. Amid the confusions of an anxious earth we meet to celebrate the Christ Child's coming. Light of the world, who didst shine that first Christmas in a dark generation, and didst come to a strange and humble place, where shepherds gathered at a manger, shine on us in our darkness, come to us in our humble estate, that while we sing of our Lord's birth long ago, our hearts may rejoice because his Spirit has been born anew in us.

We need thy strengthening presence to sustain us through these troubled days, and to keep unspoiled the Christlike spirit of good will amid violence and hate. Thanks be to thee for all the happy and cleansing memories of Christmas, for the renewed faith they bring in friendship's fidelity and love's power, for names recalled of old and young upon whose remembrance we praise thee for affection given us more than we deserved. For those who long ago made Christmas beautiful; for little children, like the child whom Christ put in the midst of his disciples; and for all true friends, whose affection and faithfulness have sustained us, we thank thee at Christmas time.

We pray for the welfare of the world. Upon all who seek it grant wisdom and determination, patience and final triumph. Give to the world in our time, O God, a fresh evidence of thy victorious power! Let the angels' song of good will among men come down from heaven to earth, and be the song of the nations too. May he who came first as a little child come now as more than a child—the Savior, victor over sin and death and hell, the redeemer of the world and the Prince of Peace.

Especially for all homes we pray in every nation under heaven, for all mothers who cradle their infants, for all hungry children, all unwanted children, for the innocent upon whom fall the iniquities of the world, for them we pray. And as we pray, may we give! Enlarge our sympathies, and with our generous support may thy missionaries be enabled to carry the ministry of thy Church to the ends of the earth. Today when we joyfully call Christ, "Lord, Lord," may we remember his warning, and do the will of his Father in heaven.

Now visit those especially in this company who feel beyond the reach of the radiance that Christmas brings; bereaved, tempted, and perplexed, in whatsoever ill estate we be, let thy strength be sufficient for us now. Come to us in some unexpected insight, some invasion of unlooked-for power, and work thy transforming miracle in our hearts, faith for fear, courage for cowardice, strength for weakness, victory for defeat. Increase our confidence in thee, burnish again our ideals that the fingers of the world have tarnished, give us brave hearts, and send us, who came here with plumes shorn and armor dented, into the world again rearmed with faith and strength for tomorrow's battles.

We pray in the Spirit of Christ. AMEN.

Christmas Sunday [2]

ETERNAL SPIRIT, the light of all our seeing, we lift our hearts in reverence to thee. We come to thee because we need tranquillity and strength. O thou from whom come all courage and certainty, today let the fretful anxieties of time be seen in the large horizons of the abiding. So grant that our worship may beget in us calmness of spirit, wisdom of insight, depth of intuition, certainty about thee, that shall make us strong through the days to come.

For all light and loveliness that shine upon our lives we bless thee, but, above all, for the Babe of Bethlehem. With humble footsteps and reverent hearts we come to the manger of the Child. Lead us away from our pride and conceit to the humility of childlikeness today. May the Kingdom of heaven belong to us because in spirit we have become teachable as children.

Grant thy gracious care upon our homes. If some household here feels the foundations of the family shaken, let the spirit of Christ's birthday save that home before it be too late. O God, who didst trust thy Son to a loyal family, save us from our selfishness and irascibilities, and make our homes worthy of a Christchild.

We thank thee for the faces of young men and women long separated from us in school and college who have come back to gather with us about the family hearth and in the church's fellowship. For all temptations conquered in these days behind, for all upbuilding of personality and strengthening of mind, we bless thee; for all noble purposes chosen, for all sins overcome, we thank thee. We beseech thee that in this renewed fellowship in the home and church there may come new life from thee to them and us.

Save us, O God of eternal life, from worshiping here as

though we were no more than a company of living folk upon this earth. Did not shepherds long ago hear out of the heavenlies the song of angels speaking peace? So we would have our angels, too, in the skies: the dear dead whom we have loved long since and lost awhile, who are not dead but live with thee. In homes this Christmas season where faces, that hitherto have made the house shine, are absent, God grant that nevertheless we may feel their presence, know the brush of angels' wings upon our spirits, hear their songs out of the unseen, and worship in the thought and love of them.

We pray for thy guiding hand upon our nation and all nations. So long ago the angels sang a song of peace above the fields of Bethlehem! So long tarries the day of its fulfillment! God have mercy upon us for our hatreds, our misunderstandings, for our prejudices of race and rank, color and nation, that divide us! Remind us once more that all souls are thine, that we are brothers one of another, and teach us that deep lesson of love, without learning which there is no hope for humankind.

Cross now, we pray thee, the inner thresholds of our lives and help us. Grant unto us the consolation of thy Spirit in our bereavements, the steadying of thy presence in our shaken and melancholy hours, the guidance of thy great purposes in the days of our prosperity and fortune, and in whatsoever condition of mind, body, or estate the littlest child here has come to worship, do thou come down thine own secret stair into that life and bring thy benediction.

We ask it in the name of Christ. AMEN.

A Church Anniversary Sunday

O GOD, who art, and wast, and art to come, before whose face the generations rise and pass away, age after age the living seek thee, and find that of thy faithfulness there is no end. Our fathers in their pilgrimage walked by thy guidance and rested on thy compassion. Still to their children be thou the pillar of cloud by day and the pillar of fire by night.

Take our lives one by one into thy keeping. As we worship thee, let the rising tide of thy grace fill every bay. Flood out our fear with a new faith, our cowardice with a fresh courage, our weakness with thy power, our sins with thy forgiveness; restore our souls, O Lord, and create a right spirit within us.

Eternal God, in whose name our fathers founded this church long ago, we pray that the spirit that kindled their lives may burn within us. We thank thee for every memory which this day revives of strong faith, humane service, and Christlike character, and for the cloud of witnesses from days gone by who surround our worship here. Deepen our gratitude for sacrifices made by those who have gone the King's highway before us, and who have found in thy Church refreshment and comfort, peace and restoration, challenge to service and strength to render it. Give us grace to see the need of our children, and our children's children, and let not the heritage of the gospel fail them because of our slackness or infidelity.

Almighty God, who in the former times didst lead our fathers forth into this land, give thy grace to us, their children, in this nation now, that we may prove ourselves a people mindful of thy favor and glad to do thy will. Bless our land with honorable industry, sound learning, and pure religion. Defend our liberty and preserve our unity. Save us from violence, discord, and confusion, from pride, and arrogance, and from every evil way. Fashion into one people the multitudes brought hither of many kindreds and tongues. Endue with the spirit of wisdom those whom we entrust with authority in these troublous days, to the end that there may be peace at home and that we keep an honorable place among the nations of the earth. In the time of prosperity fill our hearts with thankfulness, and in the day of disaster suffer not our trust in thee to fail.

We pray for all institutions working for the leadership of the future, especially for our schools, colleges, and churches. Forgive us that we bequeath to youth a world which our elder hands have left so bitter and distraught. May there come to the new generation some grace of insight and strength of heart from traditions which we have not altogether defaced. Upon some young life here this day lay thou thy hand in high vocation, and call him or her into the leadership of the future.

We pray thee for this church. May its enlarging past be an encouragement to the present and a prophecy of the future. For thy Church throughout all the world we pray, set today amid the perplexities of a changing order, and face to face with new tasks. Make us and all churches true homes of the Divine Spirit, fruitful sources of great character, and an inspiration to world-wide service. For little children who enter these doors, for youths who seek here their inspiration, for all homes whose roots are in the sanctuary, for this company, and all absent friends whose prayers are with us, we lift our supplication. Make us, O God, worthy of thy Church, and make thy Church worthy of thy Christ. AMEN.

A National Anniversary

GOD OF OUR FATHERS, their stay in trouble, their strength in conflict, their guide and deep resource, we worship thee. Be thou to us what our fathers have said thou wert to them, a fortress, a high tower, a refuge in the day of trouble. We, too, are tossed about by the vicissitudes of life and the uncertainties of fate. We need security. We long for peace. We would find the things that endure. We need strength greater than our own.

Our fathers have said that thou wert to them a pillar of cloud by day and of fire by night, that thou didst lead them, thy word a lamp unto their feet and a light unto their path. Be that to us. We, too, are pilgrims and pioneers still launching out on stormy seas for lands unknown. Each day is an adventure. O God of the pilgrims and pioneers, lead us in paths of righteousness for thy name's sake.

Our fathers have said concerning thee that thou wert to them the captain of the well-fought fight, that thou, the Lord of Hosts, didst gird them with the armor of the Lord and arm them with the sword of the Spirit. Be that to us. We, too, must fight. Contentions rise up within us, and adverse circumstances rear themselves hostilely against us, and we need the courage that our fathers knew. Be thou to us the Captain of the Host. And at the end of the long day grant that we, too, may say, I have fought a good fight.

Our fathers said thou wert their friend, the unseen companion of their pilgrimage, in whom with utter trust they could confide. Be that to us. We, too, need friendship. Blessed be thy name for earthly friends who by their love make life beautiful. Yet the day comes when we would see through earthly friendship into the divine care, and feel the everlasting arms beneath us. O Father of the faithful, in the day of need we, too, like our fathers before us, would speak unto thee as a man speaketh with his friend.

God of our fathers, we pray thee today for the nation that the fathers founded. We thank thee for the heritage that has come down to us, bought by other toil and other tears than ours. For great character, that has been woven into the fabric of this nation, blessed be thy name! For great leaders whom in crucial times thou hast lifted up to direct our paths, blessed be thy name! Help us today with vivid vision to see the heroes of old who feared thy name. Steady our hands to grasp the torch of the nation's righteousness, which they bequeathed to us. Make stable and wise our minds to understand the high entrustment, that the light of this people may not fail.

Be with the nation's schools. Upon the boys and girls who there prepare to take the place of the older generation let thy special blessing rest. We have not handled our generation's life so well that we can be proud of it. See how our wars have devastated human life! Grant that there may be more hope from those that come up from the gates of the dawn. Make them lovers of peace, lovers of concord, lovers of righteousness, for thy name's sake.

Be with the churches of the nation. Heal their dismemberments. Beget in us unity because we are drawn close to Christ and so drawn close one to another. Bring back to us the gospel of salvation for personal character and social relationships so that the Church once more may be the conscience of the nation.

So bless us and all who like us seek thy grace this day, that upon the President and all the humblest members of the commonwealth thy benediction may rest until at last to us and all other peoples may come the day of brotherhood and peace.

We ask it in the name of Christ. AMEN.

A Time of Crisis

Eternal Spirit, who art the source of all excellence, inspire us today as though the sun of a new spiritual springtime had risen upon us. Carry us out of inner darkness and gloom into light, out of our deadness of heart into life, out of our barrenness into fruitfulness and the promise of a good harvest. Thanks be to thee for thy human ministers of light and love who have acquainted us with incarnate goodness, so that our eyes have seen it and our lives have been redeemed by it. For mothers and fathers, we thank thee, for homes where fidelity and good will have made life beautiful, for friends whom we have loved and known, and for friends unknown, by whose multiplied service and sacrifice across the ages a great heritage has come to us. Make us worthy of this high company of the world's servants and saviors.

We need thee in our troubles, for they are many. We are burdened with the tragic sorrows of the world, with the needs and griefs of those we love, and with inner perplexities and problems that destroy our peace. We must choose between faith and fear, courage and cynicism, strength of character and collapse of life—and we would choose the better way. Therefore we seek in thee vision and power and hope. Grant us grace to accept the materials of life we must accept and to use them worthily. Open our eyes to see opportunity here where we struggle, and to be challenged and not defeated by our troubles, knowing that those who are for us are more than those who are against us.

For the world we pray, facing so great disaster that every hour is sobered by fearful premonition. O thou who didst sit king at the flood, be sovereign now as this flood threatens the world. Ours the sin that caused it, we confess. Grant us patience to endure; fortitude that having done all we may stand; let us lift by our faith and not depress by our discouragement. Grant wisdom to those upon whom rest the nation's responsibilities; and so overrule the waywardness of man that doors may open where we had thought all escape was ended, and peace come at last with promise of justice and humane decency and freedom.

Especially we commend to thy care thy Church, and ourselves as members of her fellowship. Keep us faithful to Christ in these days that tempt us to apostasy. Let us not trust Satan to cast out Satan! Help us above the world's violence to see Christ still the hope of our world. Lo, how we crucify him afresh—yet will he rise again!

Deepen, we beseech thee, our appreciation of the opportunities that face us in this troubled time. God forgive us that so often we ask for comfort and ease. Teach us the high meanings of hardship and adversity. Beget in us the spirit of our pilgrim sires who dared the wintry ocean and were not afraid. Make us worthy of the fathers and mothers that were before us and send us out grateful that thou hast not called us into a finished world but into an earth unfinished that we might bear a hand with thee in its completion.

O God, who canst not make a good world out of evil men and women, cleanse our hearts, forgive our sins, and amend our ways. Grant that in this place where we have come to worship thee thy transforming grace may change our lives. Turn us from the grudges we have borne, the unbrotherliness we have practiced, the uncleanness we have harbored, the selfishness we have clung to. May we go forth a more fit body of thy good soldiers to fight for righteousness.

In the name and Spirit of Christ we pray. AMEN.

In the Event of War

ETERNAL GOD, without whom life has no spiritual source, no divine meaning, purpose, or destiny, but with whom there is power for the present and hope for the future, we seek thee. So our fathers before us have sought thee in their hour of need. Refresh our faith that the strains of life may not break our spirits. Renew our courage that life's dangers and disappointments may not intimidate our souls. Amid the tumult of these days restore our confidence that our world is undergirded by thine eternal purpose. And if upon our lives such sorrow falls that happiness departs, grant us still a strong serenity, a secure trust, and a quiet peace.

Thanks be to thee for all the strength of character, the capacity for sacrifice, the courage, the forgetfulness of self, the loyalty even unto death, that in these days refresh our faith not only in thee, but in the possibilities of man. O God, lay thy strong hand upon these noble qualities which we perversely use for the world's destruction, and turn them by thy grace to redeeming ends, to build a decent and fraternal earth.

Thanks be to thee for the rich heritage of our past, for the personalities who have inspired and led us, for the ideals of liberty and democracy that have gone before us, a pillar of cloud by day and of fire by night, and for the manifold blessings of our country made sacred by the sacrifices of our sires. We pray for her with full hearts and for our sons and daughters who represent her near and far. God make America a blessing in the midst of the earth.

We come to thee, carrying in our hearts the deep affections of fathers and mothers, wives and husbands, sons and daughters, and lifting to thee with desires no words can utter, our care for those whose lives are more precious to us than our own. We come as patriots, our nation's welfare dear to us, grateful for its best traditions, anxious for its present perilous estate, prayerful for its sons now scattered over all the earth, and crying for wisdom in its leaders that we may contribute worthily to mankind's abiding peace.

For the world's sake we pray for our churches, our homes, our schools, our leaders bearing their momentous responsibility, and for us the nation's citizens, that the power committed to our country, being wisely used, may lead us not through pride to desert thy purposes, but through humble obedience to thy will to peace and security and hope for all mankind.

O God who like the ocean art not only vast but near, close to our souls as the lapping waters about the shores of an island, be near to us today. We need help. Those whom we love are in dangerous places. The news of death grows frequent and familiar. We are cast into strange places, met with heavy strains, burdened by poignant griefs. We are called on for tasks beyond our unaided strength, beset with temptations that defeat our weak resolves. We need cleansing and forgiveness, reinforcement and faith restored, that we may rise more than conquerors above the evils of the world, undaunted by its dangers and adequate for its opportunities. So meet our need today, and be to us as to our fathers our strength and hope and victory.

We pray in the Spirit of Christ.   AMEN.

A Time of Economic Distress

ETERNAL SPIRIT, never far from any one of us but often by our insensitive spirits unrecognized, we worship thee. We live not alone in a world of things beneath us which we can look down upon and so command, but in a world of appreciation and admiration, of adoration and worship. Lift us, we beseech thee, into those loftier altitudes of the spirit where we are aware of things superior and divine which we may not command because they ought to command us, nor master because by them we should be mastered.

Grant, we pray thee, that, by whatever name we call thee, or though we call thee by no name at all, every soul in thy presence may find the Divine and by the Divine be found, and so be elevated and cleansed, unified and empowered.

Speak to us through the greatness of this universe in which thou hast housed us like royal children in a palace. Let nature work her reverent awe upon us, with her vastness, her law-abiding endurance, her prodigal richness, her infinite possibilities, that we, the children of a little day upon this earth, finding ourselves in such perspectives and horizons, may grow quiet and be still.

Speak to us through beauty. Let some harmony tranquilize our souls, some thought or word of loveliness allure us so that the ugliness of life, by which we have been obsessed, may sink from view and over all may rise the excellent and the beautiful! O God, reorient some lives in thy presence to-day around those treasures of the spirit, faith in which makes life abundant and serving which enriches life indeed.

Speak to us also through some worthy purpose. Rescue us from our split and scattered lives, our futile aimlessness, our cynicism, and our disbelief. Let our eyes rest this day upon some noble purpose that, running through the channel of our lives like a great river, may gather from every side the tributaries of our faith and service. Unite some heart in thy presence to serve thee.

Yet here in the quiet of thy sanctuary we would not escape from life. Lo, how the silence of this place is populous with sound—the echoes of the footsteps of those who look for work and cannot find it, the cries of mothers anxious for their children's food! Disturb us, we beseech thee, by sounds of grief from the world outside. Let no one of us rest content, but make us penitent for our social evils, for our greed, selfish ambition, and carelessness of one another's good. O God, give us the grace to open some channels by which thy saving strength can come into the hearts of thy people. Grant us a new and holy indignation against social wrong, and, above all, thy triple gift of faith and wisdom and courage.

Beyond our power to speak the needs of all, we lift in secret prayer the intimate and domestic wants of our lives in personal character and in family relationships. There are griefs here to be comforted, anxieties to be assuaged, prosperity that should not make us proud, difficulty that should not cast us down, temptation that we should rise above, and burdens that ought to call out in us power and not bitterness. O God, according to the riches of thy grace, minister thou to the intimate needs of thy people.

In the Spirit of Christ. AMEN.

Funeral Service of a Loyal Christian

ETERNAL SPIRIT, from whom we come, to whom we belong, and in whose service is our peace, even in the presence of death our first word to thee is thanks for thine unnumbered mercies. For the memory of loved ones now departed, in whom we have seen the light of thy presence, we thank thee. For victories of character over trial, of courage over difficulty, of faith over sorrow, and for all souls who have done justly, loved mercy, and walked humbly with their God, we are grateful unto thee. Grant us now such spiritual triumph in the memory of our friend, thy servant, in whose character and long years of service we rejoice, that in our hearts death may be swallowed up in victory.

Thou art the God of the living. With thee there is no death. Our departed who have passed out of our sight are at home with thee forevermore. As thou didst not lose them in giving them to us, so have we not lost them by their return to thee. Deepen in us this faith in life eternal.

Our Father, we need strong comfort amid the perplexities and sorrows of this, our difficult, mysterious pilgrimage. Lead us to the high hills from which alone our help comes. Around our transiency and our vicissitude throw the horizons of thine everlastingness. Comfort us, not only with thy nearness but with thy greatness, O thou, who from everlasting to everlasting art God.

Thanks be to thee for all great seers and saints of the past, prophets and apostles, servants of the common good, through whom thou hast shined like the sun through eastern windows to make this earth more beautiful. Thanks be to thee for humbler souls, whom we have known and loved long since and lost awhile, who in the circle of our homes and friend-ships were to us like wayside springs on our dusty pilgrimage, or like the comfortable shade of some familiar tree. Here in the presence of death we would remember their life and thank thee for every revelation of friendliness and strength that through them has illumined us. O Lord, who art the God of the living, make real to us now the fellowship of the Unseen World. People our hearts with the saving presence of the souls invisible, and teach us afresh that life is ever lord of death and that love can never lose its own.

Let thy mercy rest upon us, a company of friends, who today remember with grateful affection thy servant who has departed this life. For his uprightness of character, for his fidelity and loyalty, thanks be to thee! For his devotion to his family, his generous good will to his friends, his patriotism as a citizen, and his high honor as a man, thanks be to thee! For the long years of able service which he rendered to thy Church and to many a Christian cause, we thank thee. Give especially to those who most intimately mourn his going wide margins of comfort around their spiritual need and deep wells to draw their consolation from.

Once more we stand upon the shore of the sea and bid farewell to a ship that loses itself over the rim of the world. O God, give fair voyaging and safe harbor! And as we stand upon this hither shore and bid farewell, grant us faith to hear the voices which on yonder shore cry, "Welcome!" and "All hail!"

"O Lord, support us all the day long of our troublous life, until the shadows lengthen and the evening comes and the busy world is hushed and the fever of life is over and our work is done. Then in thy mercy grant us a safe lodging and a holy rest and peace at the last."

We pray in the Spirit of Christ. AMEN.

LITANIES

A Litany of the Cross

Minister: O God of grace and glory, we acknowledge before thee our unpayable indebtedness; we are the children of sacrifice; our choicest benedictions have been bought with the price of other blood and tears than our own; thou hast given us the inheritance of them that feared thy name.

Response: O Lord, make us thankful.

Minister: For all saints and martyrs, prophets and apostles; for all soldiers of the common good who served thee in scorn of consequence and fell on sleep unashamed, of whom the world was not worthy,

Response: O Lord, make us thankful.

Minister: For the Cross of Christ and his exceeding bitter sacrifice; for the truths which there were brought to light, the love unbounded which there was freely given, and the costly salvation which there visited thy people,

Response: O Lord, make us thankful.

Minister: By his loneliness in the Garden; by his betrayal and his trial; by the humiliation of his people's hate, the mockery of his thorny crown, and the bitterness of scourging; by the anguish of his Cross; by his unfailing faith in thee and love for man,

Response: O Lord, make us thankful.

Minister: Eternal God, may we, who owe our spiritual blessings to so great a cloud of witnesses, who have suffered before us, and to Christ, whose Cross is our peace, walk as becomes those who are debtors to thy grace. From ingratitude, pride, hardness of heart, and all manner of evil requiting,

Response: Good Lord, deliver us.

Minister: From neglect of blessings dearly purchased; from selfish use of opportunities for which good men died; from growing within our hearts the venomous roots of covetousness; from pampering ourselves with vain super-fluities; and from all spendthrift wasting of our costly heritage,

Response: Good Lord, deliver us.

Minister: Gird us, we beseech thee, with gratitude and fidel-ity; devote us to the service of mankind with more cour-ageous zeal; free us from the detaining reluctance of our fear, selfishness, and unbelief; and at this Altar of Re-membrance, may we, O Christ, join afresh the honorable company of thy true servants who in sacrificial living share the fellowship of thy Cross.

Response: Lord, have mercy upon us and grant us this bless-ing. AMEN.

A New Year's Litany

Minister: O God, who inhabitest eternity, whose name is holy, with hushed spirits in the quiet of thy sanctuary we wait the closing moment of another year.

Response: We lift up our hearts unto thee, O Lord.

Minister: From the failures of the past, from broken hopes and disappointed ambitions, from our sins against ourselves and against others, and from the transiency and vicissitude of our lives,

Response: We lift up our hearts unto thee, O Lord.

Minister: We confess the unworthy living that has stained the record of the year that now is dying. For pardon, for grace to make restitution, for a clean heart and a right spirit with which to enter the new year,

Response: We lift up our hearts unto thee, O Lord.

Minister: Grant us honesty to face ourselves before we confront another twelvemonth. Save us from self-deceit, mean excuses, unworthy evasions, and prepare us with inner integrity and spiritual resource, that we may be adequate for all that lies before us.

Response: Lord, have mercy upon us and grant us this blessing.

Minister: From loss of faith and hope and courage, from anxiety that harasses us, fear that affrights us, cowardice that defeats us, and from the loss of thy companionship, without which no life is good, no soul is strong,

Response: Good Lord, deliver us.

Minister: From cherishing ill will in a world that perishes for want of good will, from selfishness in a world whose need of generosity and magnanimity is deep and desperate, from so living that Christ shall be crucified again and the Kingdom of God delay its coming,

Response: Good Lord, deliver us.

Minister: Confirm now in each of us some worthy decision. Bring us to the new year's beginning with such vision of our duty, such resolution to perform it, and such resources for its consummation that whether in this year ahead we live or fall on sleep, we shall be undishonored and un-ashamed before thee.

Response: Lord, have mercy upon us and grant us this bless-ing. AMEN.

A Litany of the Home

Minister: O God, who settest the solitary in families, we lift before thee the dear and sacred interests of our homes.

Response: We beseech thee to hear us, O Lord.

Minister: Make our families radiant centers of joy and schools of character. Grant unto those who wed true love and loyalty; grant unto parents, for their children's sake, the persuasiveness of good and faithful lives; grant unto youth the gladness that has no bitter fruit and integrity that need not be ashamed.

Response: We beseech thee to hear us, O Lord.

Minister: Deliver us from the spiritual foes of our households, from mean and peevish tempers, from envy of others' goods, from petulant moods and nagging tongues, and from all loveless and disloyal dealing whereby marriage is despoiled of glory and childhood of its chance.

Response: We beseech thee to hear us, O Lord.

Minister: We rejoice in memories of the dear and holy dead who live unto thee in thy house of many mansions; by their love, cherished in our hearts, may thy love grow more real, and by their death may heaven become more homelike to our imagining. Make their remembered presence a hallowed shrine for our thought and their unfailing love a sacrament where we hold tryst with thee. O God, from whom every family in heaven and on earth is named, save us from betrayal of the great love wherewith our homefolk have loved us.

Response: We beseech thee to hear us, O Lord.

Minister: For the nation's sake, whose foundations are in the family, we pray for the homes of our people. From marriage vows lightly planned, carelessly plighted, and trivially broken,

Response: Good Lord, deliver us.

Minister: From public evils which impoverish households, degrade childhood, cheapen love, and dishonor old age,

Response: Good Lord, deliver us.

Minister: O Christ, who hast called God Father and all men brethren, give us thy spirit of good will and fidelity that we may build homes with the shadow of the Almighty for their covering defense; within their shelter may tranquillity abide and joy abound; may Christian faith and fruitful character find there congenial soil; may the world's vulgarity and selfishness cease at their peaceful door; and from them may the zeal of youth and the strength of maturity go forth to make at last the whole earth a home and all mankind one family.

Response: Lord have mercy upon us and grant us this blessing. AMEN.

A Litany of Aspiration

Minister: O God, who hast so curiously made us that from whatever heights we climb we see yet loftier heights before and, forever being thus dissatisfied, behold what we ought to be outreaching what we are, strengthen in us this divine discontent.

Response: We lift up our hearts unto thee, O Lord.

Minister: From all manner of self-complacency, from pride in the actual and forgetfulness of the ideal, from the cowardice of time-serving and the contented living of mediocre lives on common levels,

Response: We lift up our hearts unto thee, O Lord.

Minister: We confess our temptation to measure our lives by the standards of the crowd and to excuse our disordered behavior by appeal to common practices. O Christ, who didst demand of thy disciples, "What do ye more than others?" grant us such clarity of vision, independence of mind, and courage of will that we may live according to our best conscience, without fear or favor of the multitude.

Response: We lift up our hearts unto thee, O Lord.

Minister: Grant us humility, knowing that we have not yet attained; shame us from our pride by a fresh vision of our possibilities; and since what we are is but the seed of what we may grow to be, grant us the inspiration of his Spirit, who gives to them that receive him power to become the sons of God.

Response: Lord, have mercy upon us and grant us this blessing.

Minister: Disturb us with visions of a juster social order. From being contented ourselves while poverty and ignorance, lack of labor, and destitution of soul afflict our fellows,

Response: Good Lord, deliver us.

Minister: From complacency with political corruption, racial prejudice, the hardships of unfair industry, the disunion of the churches, and the insanity of war,

Response: Good Lord, deliver us.

Minister: O God, who without our asking it hast set us in this mysterious scheme of circumstance, give us light in the same that we may know the path to walk in. Confirm in us the dreams of seers and the hopes of prophets; let not cynicism blight nor faithlessness uproot our confidence in thy coming Kingdom of righteousness upon the earth; and at the fire of our faith let courage be kindled that we may live as we pray.

Response: Lord, have mercy upon us and grant us this blessing. AMEN.

A Litany of Obedience

Minister: O God, who art of too pure eyes to behold iniquity and before whom transgressors cannot stand, deliver us from our self-deceits and mean excuses, and give us grace to see and acknowledge our sins before our own souls and thee.

Response: Spirit of God, descend upon my heart.

Minister: We have been careless, cowardly, mutinous; by base imaginings and vindictive broodings, by carnal passions and selfish dealings, by harsh tempers and unlovely manners, we have wronged our own hearts and hurt our fellows.

Response: Spirit of God, descend upon my heart.

Minister: We remember before thee in the house of prayer neglected virtues that would have adorned our own souls, gladdened our friends, bettered the world, and contented thy Spirit.

Response: Spirit of God, descend upon my heart.

Minister: From all claiming of faith while we have not works; from taking comfort in the luxury of thy grace while we forget the necessity of thy righteousness,

Response: Good Lord, deliver us.

Minister: From infirmity of purpose, slackness of indifference, and all moral deadness of heart,

Response: Good Lord, deliver us.

Minister: Write thine ancient law upon our hearts:
Thou shalt have no other gods before me.

Thou shalt not bow down thyself to them, nor serve them.

Thou shalt not take the name of the Lord thy God in vain.

Remember the sabbath day, to keep it holy.

Honor thy father and thy mother.

Thou shalt not kill.

Thou shalt not commit adultery.

Thou shalt not steal.

Thou shalt not bear false witness against thy neighbor.

Thou shalt not covet.

Response: Lord, have mercy upon us and incline our hearts to keep this law.

Minister: Above all, bring to our remembrance thy new teaching: the whole law is fulfilled in this that a man should love his neighbor as himself.

Response: Lord, have mercy upon us and write all these thy laws in our hearts, we beseech thee.   AMEN.

A Litany of the Nation

Minister: O God, before whose face the empires of the past have risen and fallen away, establish this nation in righteousness; and in personal character and public integrity make her foundations sure.

Response: Lord, hear our prayer and mercifully bless this people.

Minister: From the ravages of crime, the disgrace of political corruption, and all malicious designs of lawless men,

Response: Good Lord, deliver us.

Minister: From prejudice of race and color, making schism in the commonwealth; from all inequity that, causing a few to be rich and many poor, begets ill will and spoils fraternity; from loss of liberties bequeathed us by our sires and from careless acceptance of our heritage and neglect of its responsibilities,

Response: Good Lord, deliver us.

Minister: From the decline of pure religion, from failure of moral fiber in our citizenship, from all accounting of things material above virtues spiritual; from vulgarity of life, loss of social conscience, and collapse of national character,

Response: Good Lord, deliver us.

Minister: By the deep faiths on which the foundations of our land were laid and by the sacrifices of its pioneers,

Response: We beseech thee to hear us, O Lord.

Minister: By the memory of leaders in the nation, whose

wisdom has saved us, whose devotion has chastened us, whose characters have inspired us,

Response: We beseech thee to hear us, O Lord.

Minister: By the undeserved wealth of a great continent committed to us and by our trusteeship of power to work weal or woe on the earth,

Response: We beseech thee to hear us, O Lord.

Minister: Keep us from pride of mind, and from boasting tongues deliver us; save our national loyalty from narrowness and our flag from selfish shame; by our love for our land may we measure the love of others for their lands, honoring their devotion as we honor our own; and acknowledging thee one God, may we see all mankind one family and so govern our national affairs that the whole world may become one brotherhood of peoples.

Response: Lord, hear our prayer and mercifully bless this people. AMEN.

A Litany of Friendship

Minister: O Spirit of Grace, who hast tempered the rigor of this present world with the loveliness of friendship, we rejoice in our friends.

Response: Thanks be to thee, O Lord.

Minister: For the encouragement of their love, the support of their confidence, the faithfulness of their counsels, and the warmth of their affection,

Response: Thanks be to thee, O Lord.

Minister: For those most singular and blessed gifts of friendship—power to keep faith with our own souls; to walk cleanly amid the soil and bravely amid the disheartenment of life; to believe in our best in the face of failure, and in extremities to be of excellent hope,

Response: Thanks be to thee, O Lord.

Minister: For friends, living on earth and departed hence, whose love has been our peace and strength; for the beauty of their lives through which thou hast shined upon us like the sun through eastern windows; and for thy Christ who called us not servants, but friends,

Response: Thanks be to thee, O Lord.

Minister: Because our sins hurt not ourselves only, but our friends, we are ashamed and penitent. For hasty temper and thoughtless word, for lack of kindliness and understanding, and for all disloyal dealing, open or secret, whereby we have betrayed those who trusted us,

Response: We repent before thee, O Lord.

Minister: We stand in awe before our power to sway the lives and control the happiness of those who love us. For all misuse of friendship to untoward ends, for unbelief that mars a friend's faith, for low tastes which drag him down, for miserable moods which cloud his skies, and for all unworthy living which roughens his spiritual journey,

Response: We repent before thee, O Lord.

Minister: Because friendship is so excellent a grace, widen its domain, we beseech thee. Reclaim from violence and strife the relationships of races and nations; redeem them from suspicion and prejudice to good will and trust. O Sun of Righteousness, shine on our fierce and wayward world, and lighten its path to brotherhood.

Response: Lord, have mercy upon us and grant us this blessing.

Minister: Make our human friendships, we beseech thee, a revelation to our souls of thine unfailing love. Despite the mysterious dealings of thy Providence, the sternness of thy laws, and the severity of thy just visitations, may we walk by faith in thy friendliness. Enfold us in thy grace, support us by thy power, establish us in thy fellowship, and grant us the crown of life, that we should be the friends of God.

Response: Lord, have mercy upon us, and grant us this blessing. AMEN.

A Christmas Litany

Minister: Eternal Spirit, Father of all grace and goodness, we thank thee for the children, and at this Christmas time we bless thee for Christ's revelation of the beauty and value of childhood.

Response: Alleluia. Blessed be God, Eternal Friend of children.

Minister: For his tender compassion toward them; for his burning indignation against those who do them wrong; for his deep and overflowing love, drawing them toward himself; for his message of their nearness to the Father of all,

Response: Blessed be God.

Minister: For the loveliness of children; for their mirth and laughter; for the gladness and light they bring into the world,

Response: Blessed be God.

Minister: For their enthusiasms, their abounding energy, and their love of the heroic and adventurous; for their candid, generous trust in those around them; and for their quick response to calls of love and service,

Response: Blessed be God.

Minister: For the childhood of Jesus our Lord; for his birth and helpless babyhood; for his mother's gentle care and nurture; and for all unknown souls who nursed and tended him,

Response: Alleluia. Blessed be God, Eternal Friend of Children.

Minister: For his joyful, eager, obedient boyhood, uplifting all human childhood; for the grace and love of God, which in him were revealed and which gave to us the joy of knowing the Father,

Response: Thanks be to thee, O God.

Minister: As we give thanks for the infinite value of children, so we pray for fathers and mothers, and for all of us through whom children receive their first thoughts of God, and their early ideals of character. May we have a deepened sense of the Fatherhood of God, and may we so practice his presence, that the children may be won for goodness and beauty of life.

Response: Lord, have mercy upon us and grant us this blessing.

Minister: O Heavenly Father, make our hearts burn within us for all children who go neglected or unloved; let thy Spirit breathe into us a living renewal, that with wise statesmanship and generous philanthropy may we make of this earth a more decent and kindly place into which children may be born.

Response: Lord, have mercy upon us and grant us this blessing. AMEN.

A Litany of Joy

Minister: Eternal Spirit, who inhabitest the praises of thy people, lift us above life's anxieties and irritations into serenity and peace; give us appreciative hearts that we may keep just tally of our joys. In friendship that sustains us, patience that bears with us, mercy that forgives us, love that inspires us,

Response: We rejoice before thee, O God.

Minister: In the cleansing influence of beauty, the ennobling companionship of great books, the dear comfort of home, the sustaining strength of fair memories, and the encouragement of high hopes,

Response: We rejoice before thee, O Lord.

Minister: In the multitude of our common benedictions and in our undergirding faith in thee; in easy traveling through fair weather and in strength to sail stormy days without shipwreck; in merriment and gaiety of heart and, when these fail, in the tranquillity of thy peace,

Response: We rejoice before thee, O Lord.

Minister: From the foes of happiness within ourselves, from petulant and contentious spirits,

Response: Good Lord, deliver us.

Minister: From cynicism, self-pity, and the luxury of cheap melancholy,

Response: Good Lord, deliver us.

Minister: From anger and envy, from ingratitude and unlovely brooding, from inordinate dependence on things carnal and temporal for our joy,

Response: Good Lord, deliver us.

Minister: Grant unto us the blessedness promised to thy servants:

> Blessed are the poor in spirit, for theirs is the Kingdom of heaven.
>
> Blessed are those who mourn, for they shall be comforted.
>
> Blessed are the meek, for they shall inherit the earth.
>
> Blessed are those who hunger and thirst after righteousness, for they shall be satisfied.
>
> Blessed are the merciful, for they shall obtain mercy.
>
> Blessed are the pure in heart, for they shall see God.
>
> Blessed are the peacemakers, for they shall be called sons of God.
>
> Blessed are those who are persecuted for righteousness' sake, for theirs is the Kingdom of heaven.

Response: Lord, have mercy upon us and grant us these blessings. AMEN.

A Litany of the Tongue

Minister: O God, who hast given power to our tongues to create light or darkness in the lives of our friends, help us to keep watch over our words.

Response: Let the words of my mouth, and the meditation of my heart, be acceptable in thy sight, O Lord, my Strength and my Redeemer.

Minister: From backbiting and talebearing, from uncharitable judgment, from flattery and scandal, from deliberate lie and subtle insincerity, guard thou our wayward tongues.

Response: Let the words of my mouth, and the meditation of my heart, be acceptable in thy sight, O Lord, my Strength and my Redeemer.

Minister: We humbly confess before thee the harm done by our hasty speech. We have discouraged those we might have helped, embittered those we might have sweetened, exasperated those we might have pacified, depressed those we might have gladdened, misguided those we might have led. Convert, we beseech thee, our disordered and ill-tempered tongues.

Response: Create in me a clean heart, O God, and renew a right spirit within me.

Minister: Let all bitterness and wrath, and anger and clamor and evil-speaking be put away from us, with all malice.

Response: Create in me a clean heart, O God, and renew a right spirit within me.

Minister: Use thou our tongues for noble ends. To hearten the dismayed, illumine the benighted, strengthen the weak, comfort the sad; to bring light out of darkness, friendship out of enmity, and joy out of pain.

Response: Guide thou our lips, O Lord.

Minister: May good causes, hard bestead by many enemies, be strengthened by our forthright speech. Let not unpopularity affright us nor cowardice detain us from the stout utterance of our best convictions. May no right be denied to any man, no hopeful movement of thy purpose fail, for want of our supporting word.

Response: Guide thou our lips, O Lord.

Minister: Forasmuch as we must speak to our own hearts before we can speak to others, watch thou the inner conversation of our souls. Let not the rudder of our tongues turn the ship of our own spirits into perverse courses. Free our self-communion from every crooked way; let our inner meditation enlighten our outward speech, and may we so wisely talk to ourselves that we can persuasively talk to others.

Response: Have mercy upon us, O Lord, and grant us this blessing. AMEN.

A Litany of Praise

Minister: Spirit of God, the fountain of beauty and good-ness, from whom eternally stream all things excellent in man and nature, open our eyes to see thy wonder-working in the world and to rejoice in thee.

Response: We praise thee, O Lord.

Minister: For the constancy and beauty of thy creation; for the breath of winds, the scent of flowers, the racing clouds, the glory of the trees; for the procession of thy days and nights, the rhythm of thy seasons, and the wonder of thy stars,

Response: We praise thee, O Lord.

Minister: For all beauty in human thought and deed, for poet's song and prophet's word, the gift of music and the grace of art; for nobility of character, for the loveliness of friendship, and for the fragrance of souls nourished in thy peace,

Response: We praise thee, O Lord.

Minister: Calm our too easily disquieted spirits that they may reflect thy presence in all things excellent and of good report; take thou the dimness of our souls away. O thou who dost beset us before and behind and lay thine hand upon us, free our hearts from lethargy, our spirits from discouragement, and our lips from complaining, that we may rejoice in thee.

Response: Bless the Lord, O my soul.

Minister: For every inward intimation that we are thy chil-dren; for hours of insight when we have clearly seen thy living presence and have been persuaded of thy love; for that we cannot live by bread alone nor find rest until we rest in thee,

Response: Bless the Lord, O my soul.

Minister: For all victories of good over evil, wisdom over ignorance, love over hate, we praise thee. For ancient superstitions overpassed and ancient oppressions done away; for the evident working of thy purpose in the breaking of bondage, the enlargement of opportunity, the victories of peace, and the diffusion of light,

Response: Bless the Lord, O my soul.

Minister: For courage to endure hazard and hardship we praise thee. For the tutelage of thy Spirit teaching us how trials are to be borne off and with what answer they are to be beaten back; for spiritual valor to face life's adventure, neither seducing others, nor ourselves seduced by fear; for strength to do what is appointed and for faith to leave the unsolved mysteries in thy care,

Response: Bless the Lord, O my soul.

Minister: May all our living speak thy praise. By faithful work and wholesome play, by daily kindliness, by truthfulness of life and tongue, by secret living in thy sight and outward service for the good of man,

Response: Bless the Lord, O my soul. AMEN.

A Litany of Youth

Minister: O God, who through thy Spirit in the young Carpenter of Nazareth hast changed the face of the world and in every age dost call the fresh vigor of new life to thy service, we pray thee for the youth of our generation.

Response: We beseech thee to hear us, O Lord.

Minister: What the elders by their sin have put out of order and by their niggardliness have refused to help, strengthen the new generation with wisdom to cure and with righteousness to establish.

Response: We beseech thee to hear us, O Lord.

Minister: Guard the character of our youth and preserve their integrity against the day of thy call to service. Now in the springtime of their years may they not strip blossoms from their trees to make transient garlands of pleasure, only to find when autumn comes that there is no fruit.

Response: We beseech thee to hear us, O Lord.

Minister: From flippancy and cynicism, from deadening unbelief and purposeless living, from vulgar tastes and sensual deeds,

Response: Good Lord, deliver them.

Minister: From mistaking license for liberty, from surrender to the tyranny of undisciplined desires, from the slavery of habits which, free to begin, they are not free to stop,

Response: Good Lord, deliver them.

Minister: We praise thee for the zest and radiance of youth and for the untamed hopes with which the young continually refresh the earth, and since old customs, grown too old, corrupt the world, use thou in our time their undimmed eyes to see and their undiscouraged vigor to achieve thy will.

Response: Lord, have mercy upon us and grant us this blessing.

Minister: Enlist their unbroken strength in service of the commonweal; temper their recklessness into moral courage; out of their youthful spirit of daring bring the maturity of independent minds and venturesome endeavors; and so lead them from youth to age that, undishonored and unashamed, they may transmit to their children a better world than ours.

Response: Lord, have mercy upon us and grant us this blessing. AMEN.

A Litany for the Dedication
of an Organ

Minister: O magnify the Lord with me, and let us exalt his name together.

Response: Let us enter into his gates with thanksgiving and into his courts with praise.

Minister: Eternal Spirit, from whom stream all things excellent in man and nature, and in whose sanctuary strength and beauty dwell, we worship thee. Lift up our hearts above the harsh confusions of our time, above its din and clamor, and here refresh our souls with harmony and praise.

Response: Praise God in his sanctuary; praise him with stringed instruments and organs.

Minister: For all makers of melody, who have taught us to rejoice in song and have lifted our spirits in hymns of gratitude and praise, we thank thee. Here in thy sanctuary may music give our spirits wings, until above life's discords we hear the voices of the heavenly host, singing "Hallelujah. The Lord God Omnipotent reigneth."

Response: Let everything that hath breath praise the Lord. Praise ye the Lord.

Minister: O God of grace, grant that this instrument for thy praise, which we now dedicate, may minister to the strengthening of our faith. Here in thy sanctuary may we be reassured that life is not all dissonance and turmoil. Here may the beauty of the Lord, our God, be upon us.

Response: O sing unto the Lord a new song; sing unto the Lord, all the earth.

Minister: Upon this congregation of thy people we beseech thy blessing. May the outward harmony, with which here we worship thee, be reflected in our daily lives—in the loveliness of friendship, in fraternal concord, and in good will that heals the hurts of men and quiets their hostilities.

Response: In psalms and hymns and spiritual songs may we sing, making melody in our hearts to the Lord.

Minister: Especially we pray that since our lives are beset with hardship and our wayward spirits find duty difficult, we may here discover also the gladness of Christ's discipleship. Here may the God of hope fill us with all joy and peace in believing, until we serve the Lord with gladness and come before his presence with singing. So comfort the sorrowful, lift up the discouraged, renew the fainthearted, and teach us to say: The Lord is our strength and our song.

Response: O come, let us sing unto the Lord; let us make a joyful noise to the rock of our salvation. Let us come before his presence with thanksgiving, and make a joyful noise unto him with psalms.

Minister: As we remember our Master and his first disciples, of whom it is written, "When they had sung an hymn, they went out into the Mount of Olives," we too, being strengthened by thy Spirit, would be made ready for our difficult tomorrows. Let not our worship here be an escape from life, but a preparation for life. Here may we be so compassed about with songs of deliverance that tomorrow we may be able to do what we ought to do and to stand what we must endure.

Response: Wait on the Lord; be of good courage, and he shall strengthen thine heart. Wait, I say, on the Lord.
AMEN.